weird
but
true!
6

THAT'S WEIRD!

weird but true! 6

300 outrageous facts

NATIONAL GEOGRAPHIC
WASHINGTON, D.C.

Visit us online:
Kids: kids.nationalgeographic.com
Parents: nationalgeographic.com
Teachers: nationalgeographic.com/education
Librarians: ngchildrensbooks.org

For information about special discounts for bulk purchases, please contact National Geographic Books Special Sales: ngspecsales@ngs.org

For rights or permissions inquiries, please contact National Geographic Books Subsidiary Rights: ngbookrights@ngs.org

Paperback ISBN: 978-1-4263-1490-2
Reinforced Library Binding
ISBN: 978-1-4263-1491-9
Scholastic ISBN: 978-1-4263-1843-6

Printed in China
14/PPS/1

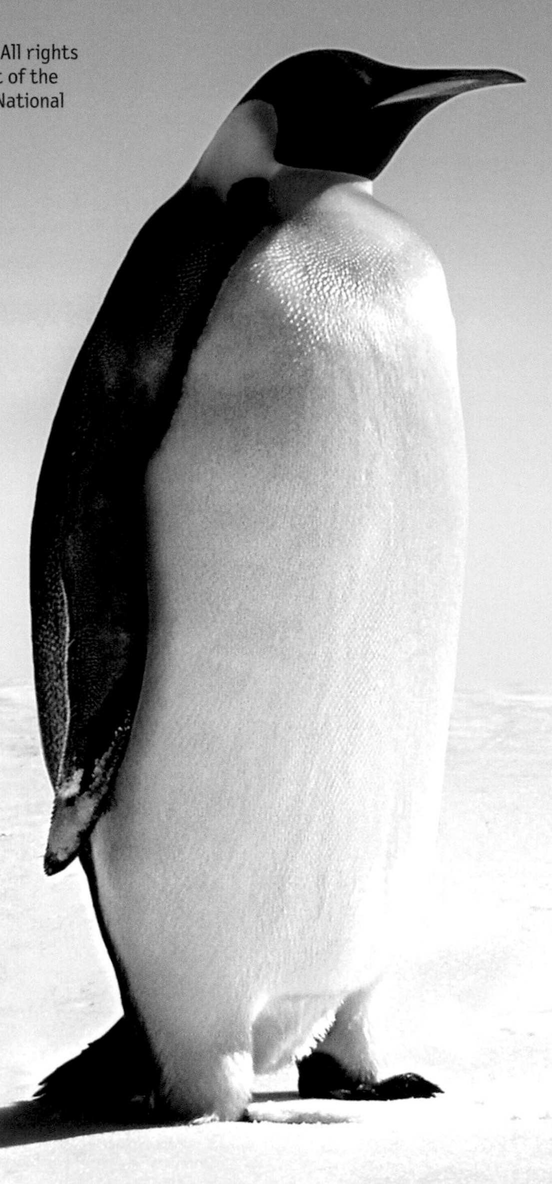

AN EMPEROR PENGUIN HAS 100 FEATHERS PER SQUARE INCH (6.5 square cm) OF ITS BODY.

THE ASIAN WEAVER ANT CAN HOLD OBJECTS 100 TIMES ITS WEIGHT— WHILE HANGING UPSIDE DOWN!

You can buy a **BACON-and-MAPLE-SYRUP-flavored LOLLIPOP.**

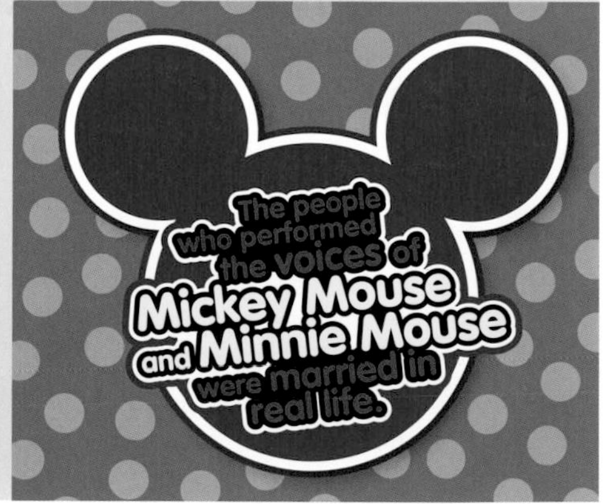

A STUDY FOUND THAT HOT CHOCOLATE TASTES SWEETER WHEN YOU DRINK IT FROM

AN ORANGE CUP VS. A WHITE CUP.

Kool-Aid can be used to clean dishwashers.

The ears of the long-eared jerboa, a nocturnal rodent, are two-thirds the size of its body.

THERE'S A
FUNGUS
THAT SECRETES
RED DROPS
THAT LOOK LIKE
BLOOD.

YOUR IRIS—THE COLORED PART OF YOUR EYE—IS AS UNIQUE AS YOUR FINGERPRINT.

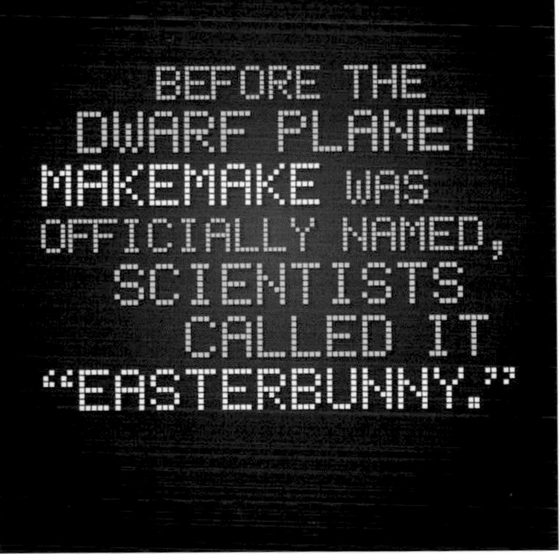

BEFORE THE
DWARF PLANET
MAKEMAKE WAS
OFFICIALLY NAMED,
SCIENTISTS
CALLED IT
"EASTERBUNNY."

PANDAS eat AS MUCH AS **36 pounds** (16 kg) OF **bamboo every day—** THAT'S AS HEAVY AS **144 hamburgers!**

THE WORLD'S LARGEST WIND TURBINE HAS BLADES THE SIZE OF A COMMERCIAL JET.

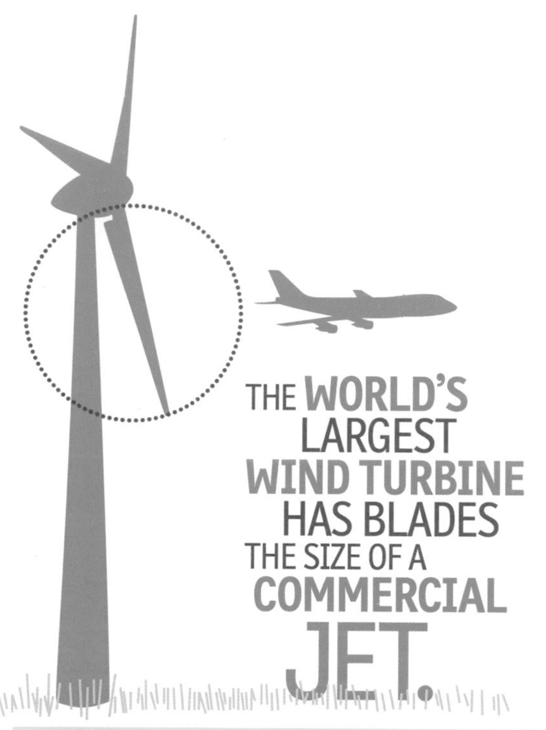

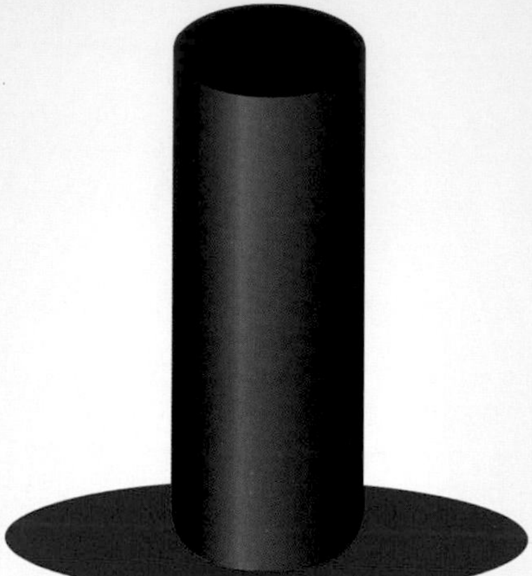

Hatshepsut, the first female pharaoh of Egypt, wore red and black nail polish.

SOME ANCIENT ROMANS RUBBED **CROCODILE DUNG** ON THEIR FACES TO SOFTEN THEIR SKIN.

For 213 years it was illegal for women to wear pants in Paris— luckily the law was never really enforced.

You'll never see a full moon and the sun in the sky at the same time.

THE JUICE OF ONE TYPE OF CHILI PEPPER CAN BURN THROUGH A LATEX GLOVE.

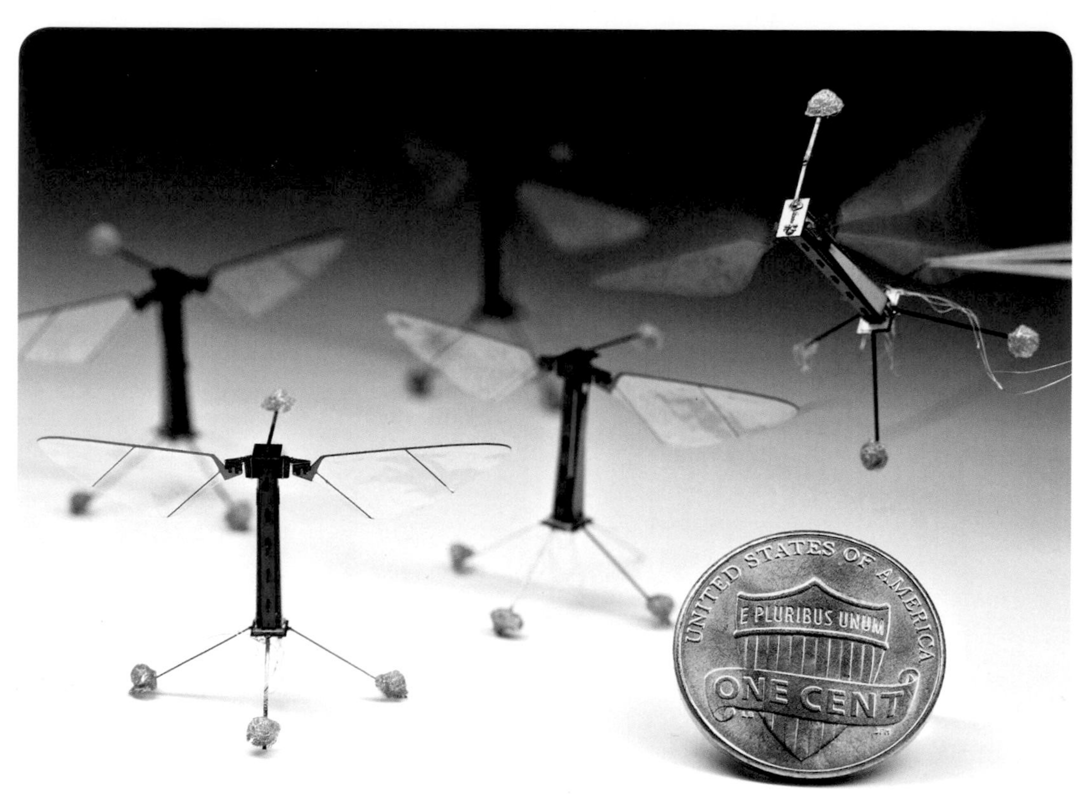

THE WORLD'S SMALLEST FLYING ROBOT

—CALLED ROBOBEE—

IS SLIGHTLY LARGER THAN A PENNY.

1.9 BILLION YEARS AGO, MUCH OF THE EARTH SMELLED LIKE ROTTEN EGGS.

The Goliath spider's fangs are as long as a paper clip.

THE SHINIEST LIVING THING ON EARTH

IS AN AFRICAN FRUIT KNOWN AS *POLLIA CONDENSATA*.

Male blue-footed boobies do a high-step strut to attract mates.

A planet partially made of diamond was calculated to be worth $26.9 nonillion (that's 26.9 plus 29 zeros)!

FOR
$100,000,
YOU CAN BUY A
KILLER WHALE-
SHAPED
SUBMARINE.

A MASS OF FLOATING ICE THAT LOOKS LIKE AN ICEBERG IS CALLED A FLOEBERG.

IF YOU ROLLED ALL THE WATER ON EARTH INTO A BALL, IT WOULD BE LESS THAN A THIRD THE SIZE OF THE MOON.

EARTH

MOON

WATER ON EARTH

The Indian
giant squirrel
has
purple
fur.

SOME **DOGS** ARE ***ALLERGIC*** TO **CATS.**

The world's largest toilet-paper pyramid was made up of 23,821 rolls.

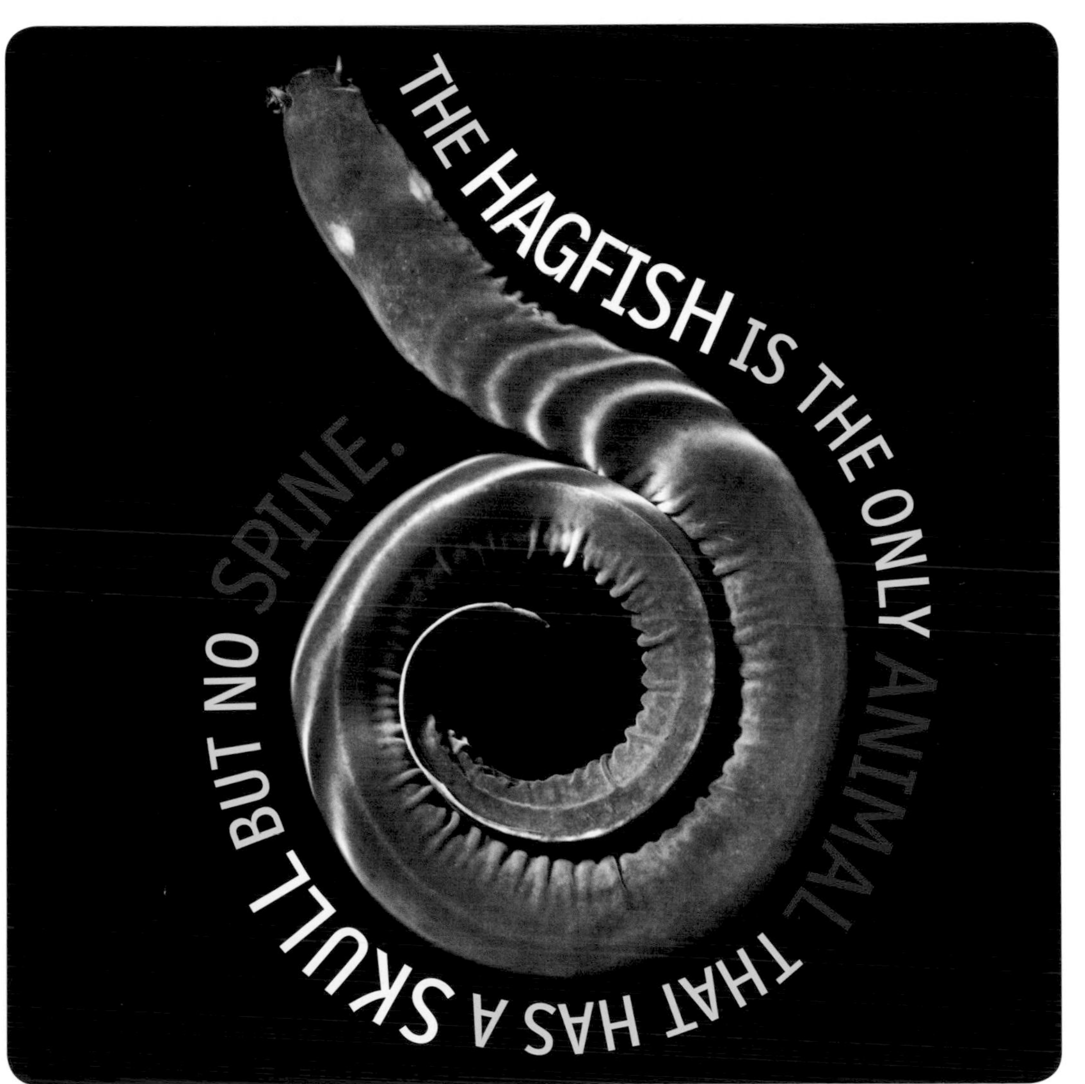
THE HAGFISH IS THE ONLY ANIMAL THAT HAS A SKULL BUT NO SPINE.

A PET RABBIT IN ENGLAND WEIGHS THE SAME AS FOUR BOWLING BALLS.

A RARE TYPE OF OCTOPUS HAS SIX ARMS.

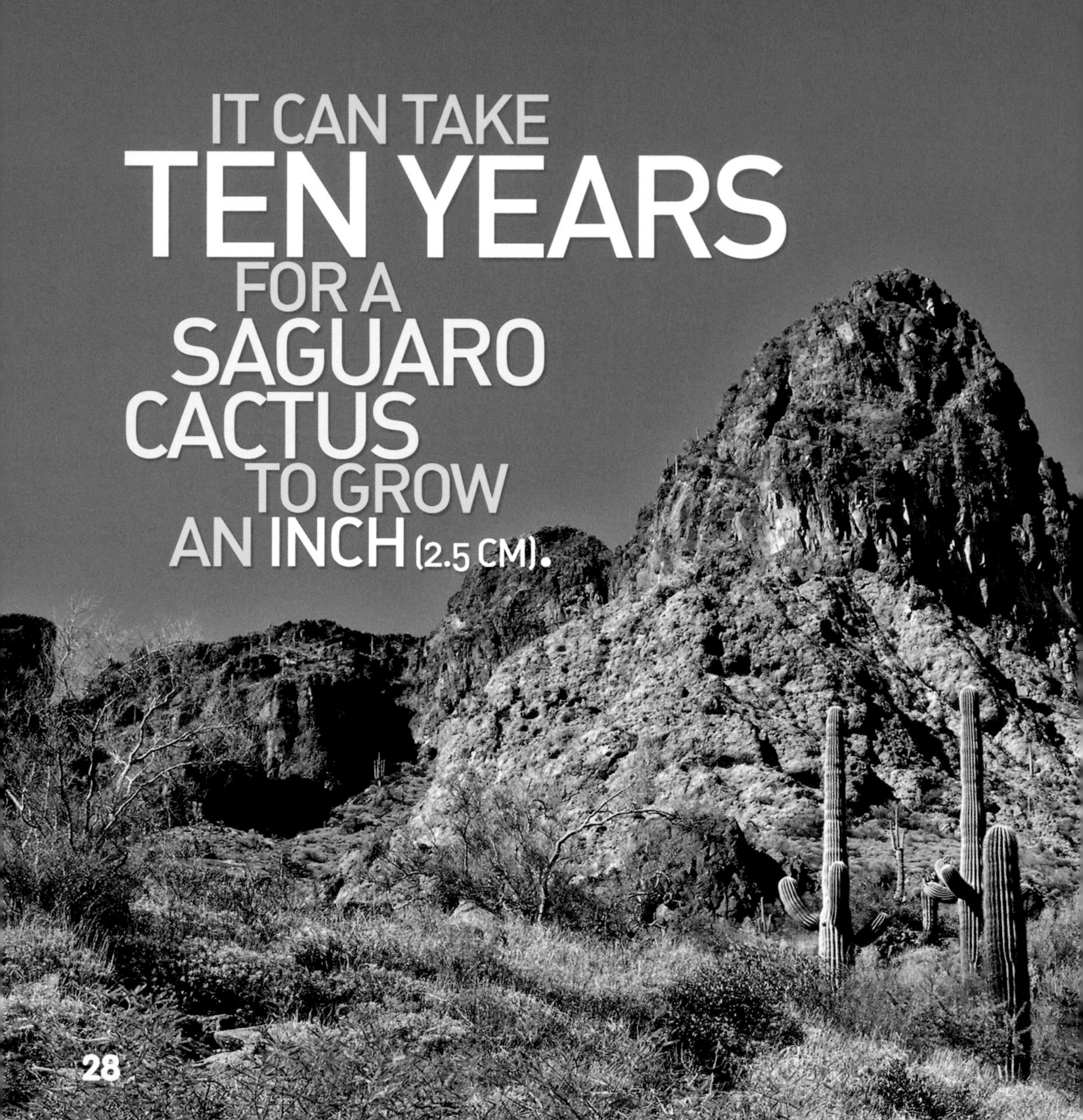

IT CAN TAKE **TEN YEARS** FOR A **SAGUARO CACTUS** TO GROW AN **INCH** (2.5 CM).

A chunk of **rock** about as long as **17,000 basketball courts** was seen floating in the South Pacific.

Ghost ants have SEE-THROUGH STOMACHS.

A PIECE OF CAKE FROM QUEEN VICTORIA'S *wedding* HAS BEEN PRESERVED IN ENGLAND FOR 174 YEARS.

A company invented a remote-controlled helicopter that's the size of a golf ball.

KOMODO DRAGONS
OFTEN VOMIT
WHEN THREATENED.

SOME PLANTS GLOW BRIGHT BLUE UNDER ULTRAVIOLET LIGHT.

MORE THAN
HALF
THE
WORLD'S
GEYSERS
ARE IN
YELLOWSTONE
NATIONAL
PARK
IN WYOMING, U.S.A.

THE NIGHT SIDE OF PLANET EARTH IS 600,000 TIMES DIMMER THAN ITS DAY SIDE.

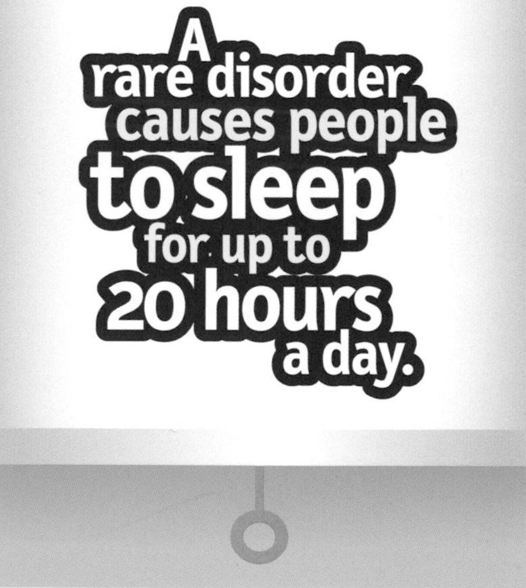

AT A STORE
IN JAPAN,
YOU CAN HAVE
A REPLICA
OF YOUR
FACE
MOLDED
INTO
CHOCOLATE.

The bee hummingbird snacks on up to 1,500 flowers a day.

A SCULPTOR CARVED A LIFE-SIZE ASTRONAUT FROM A ONE-TON BLOCK OF CHEDDAR CHEESE.

AN ASTRONAUT WROTE HIS DAUGHTER'S INITIALS ON THE DUSTY SURFACE OF THE MOON.

Some frogs eat crabs.

FOSSILS OF EARTH'S EARLIEST KNOWN ANIMALS

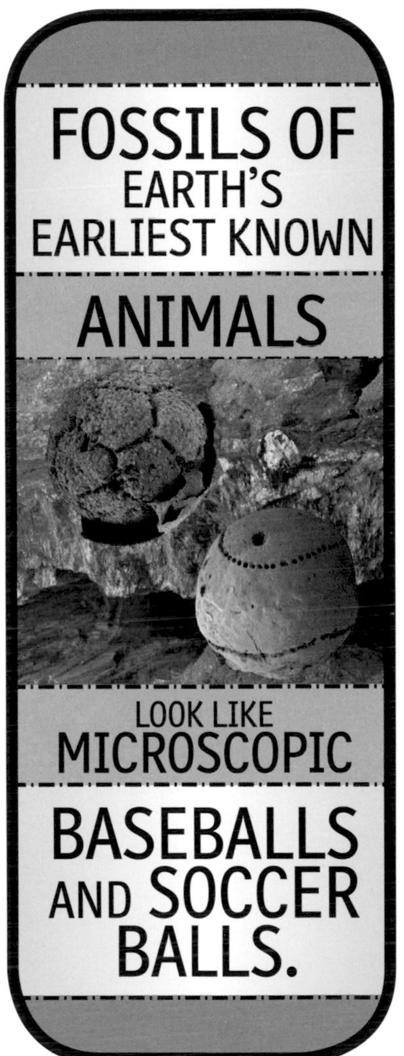

LOOK LIKE MICROSCOPIC BASEBALLS AND SOCCER BALLS.

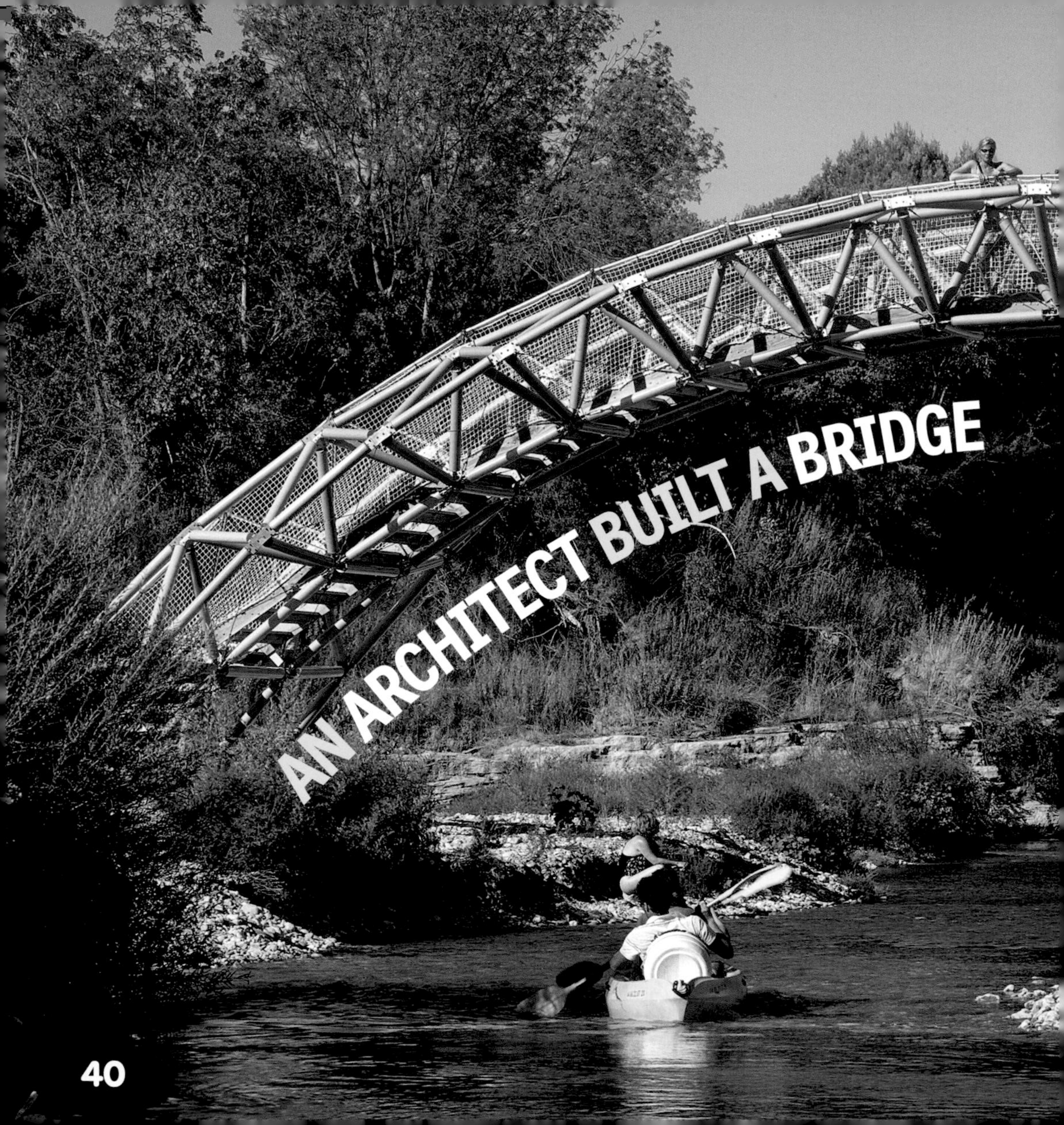

AN ARCHITECT BUILT A BRIDGE

OUT OF CARDBOARD TUBES.

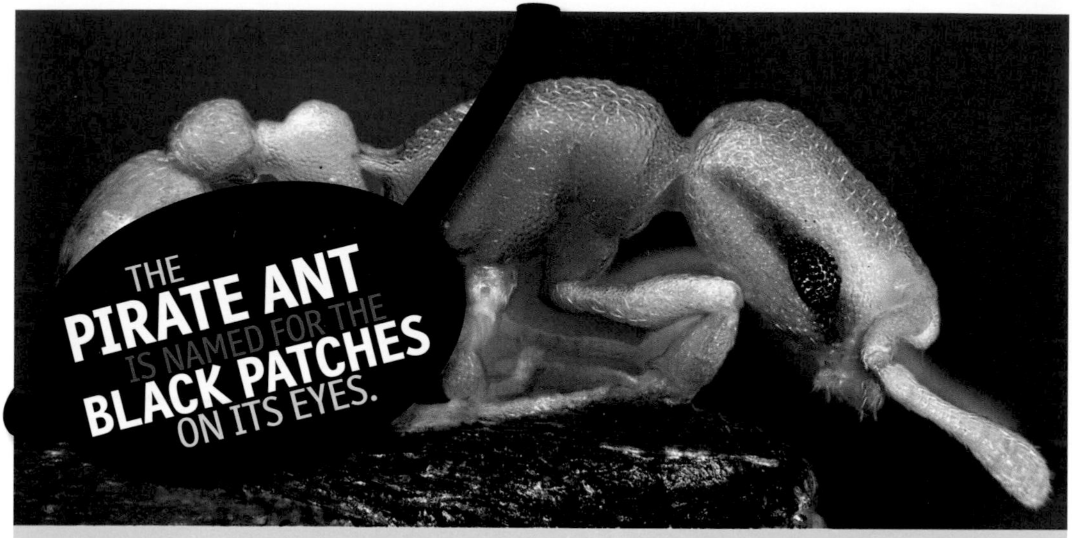

THE **PIRATE ANT** IS NAMED FOR THE **BLACK PATCHES** ON ITS EYES.

Some **catfish leap** out of the **water** to **catch pigeons** on the shore.

Female **fireflies** rarely **fly.**

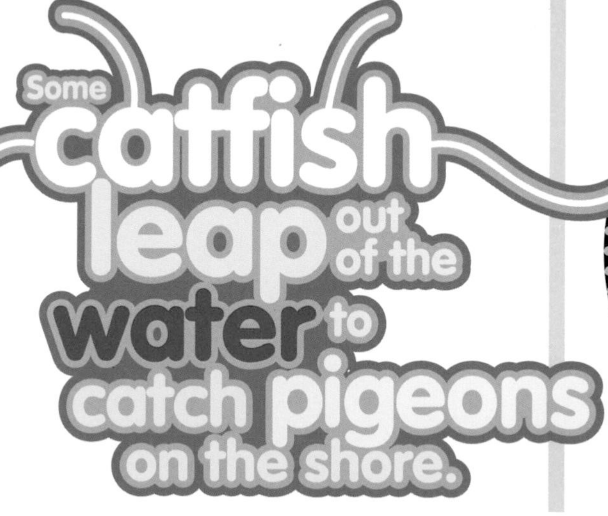

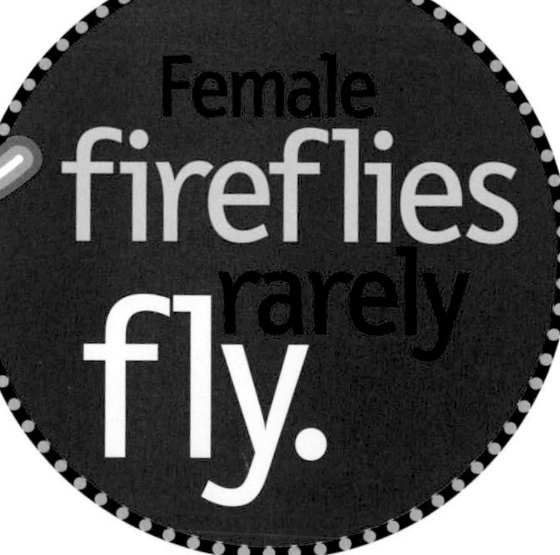

People throw away enough ribbon each year to tie a bow around the entire Earth.

Americans eat over a billion chicken wings during Super Bowl weekend.

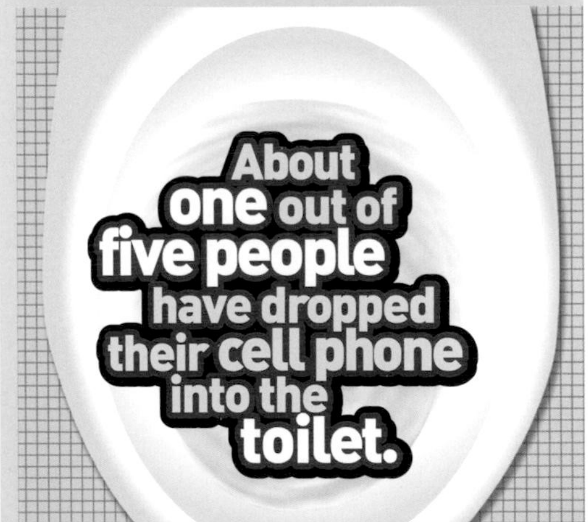

About one out of five people have dropped their cell phone into the toilet.

A LEGO SCULPTURE OF ENGLAND'S QUEEN ELIZABETH II INCLUDED A CROWN WITH REAL DIAMONDS.

Borborygmus is the word for the **rumbling sound** in your **stomach** when you're **hungry.**

Louis XIV of France wore ***four-inch-high heels.*** (10 cm)

The gray **catbird** makes a **meow** sound.

Some **green snakes** turn **blue** when they **die.**

A GORILLA AT A ZOO IN GERMANY CAN WALK ON A TIGHT-ROPE.

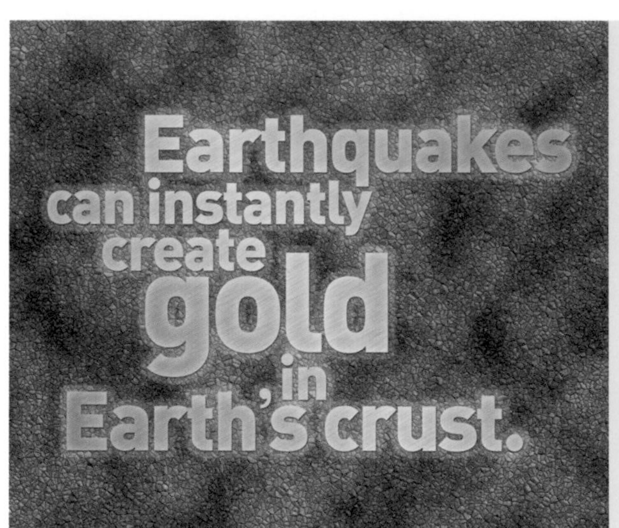
Earthquakes
can instantly
create
gold
in
Earth's crust.

An avocado
is sometimes
known as an
alligator
pear.

More
people hide
their
valuables
in their
sock drawer
than anywhere else,
according to a British study.

A SIX-CLAWED
LOBSTER
WAS CAUGHT
COUNT
THEM UP!
OFF THE COAST OF
MASSACHUSETTS,
U.S.A.

THERE'S A TOWN IN CANADA CALLED SAINT-LOUIS-DU-HA!-HA!

A WOOD FROG'S CROAK SOUNDS LIKE A QUACK.

SOME GRASSHOPPERS ARE PINK.

Scientists found that you can literally get **cold feet** when you're nervous.

IN ANCIENT GREECE, COMETS WERE CALLED "HAIRY STARS."

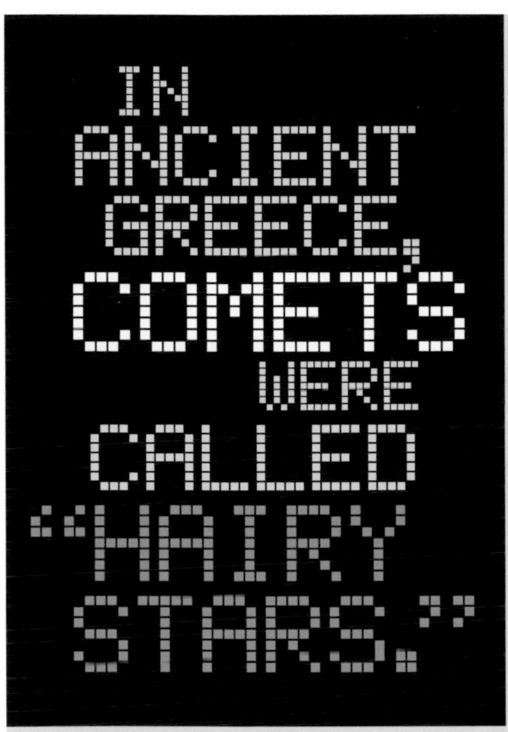

Some **house ants** smell like **fresh coconuts** when *smashed.*

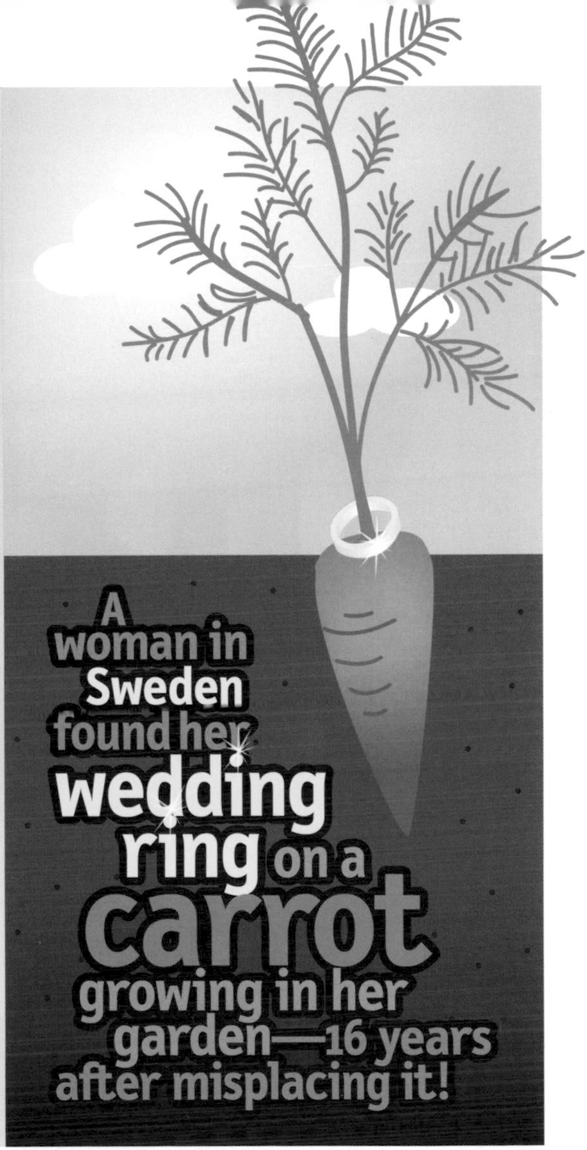

A woman in Sweden found her **wedding ring** on a **carrot** growing in her garden—16 years after misplacing it!

27 feet (8 meters)

SUNFLOWERS CAN GROW AS TALL AS TWO AFRICAN ELEPHANTS STACKED UP.

The movie *Cloudy with a Chance of Meatballs* is called *Rain of Falafel* in Israel.

IN THE WILD, **GOLDFISH** CAN GROW TO BE MORE THAN A **FOOT LONG.** (0.3 m)

A disorder called **Alien Hand Syndrome** can cause a person to **punch** and **slap himself.**

Locusts are a **popular snack** in parts of **Africa** and **Asia.**

SCANDINAVIANS IN NORWAY TRAVELED ON HANDMADE SKIS MORE THAN 6,000 YEARS AGO.

SCIENTISTS THINK THAT WATER ON THE MOON CAME FROM EARTH.

There's a road in New Jersey, U.S.A., named "Shades of Death."

A **CYCLIST INVENTED** A **BIKE HELMET** MADE FROM **RECYCLED NEWSPAPERS.**

AFRICAN LIONS CATCH ABOUT **25 PERCENT** OF THE PREY THEY CHASE.

DRAGONFLIES CATCH **95 PERCENT.**

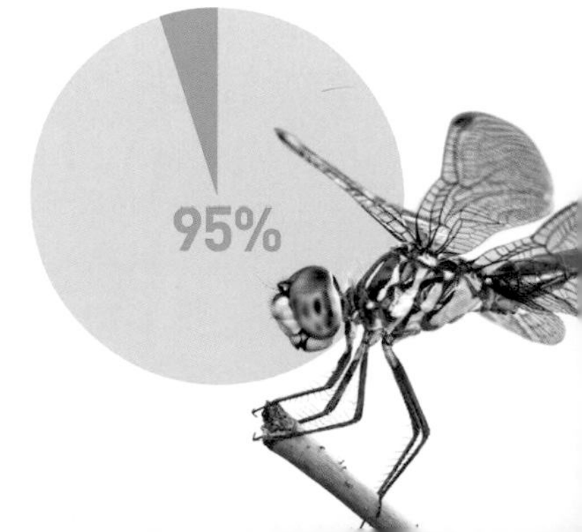

A 10-YEAR-OLD KID IS MADE UP OF ABOUT 3,200,000,000,000,000,000,000,000,000 ATOMS.

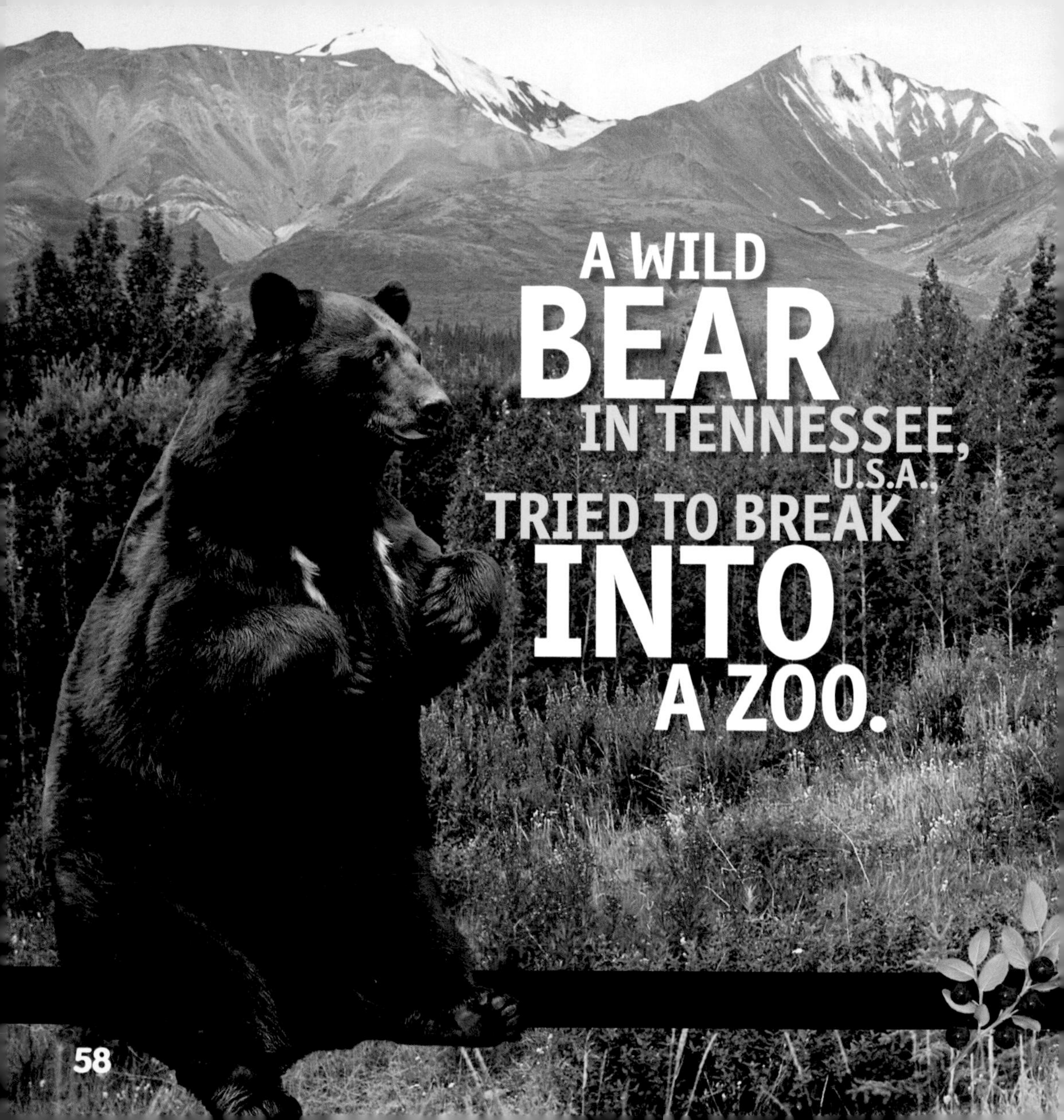

A WILD BEAR IN TENNESSEE, U.S.A., TRIED TO BREAK INTO A ZOO.

THERE IS ABOUT **ONE BEAR** FOR EVERY **TWO PEOPLE** IN THE YUKON TERRITORY, CANADA.

A GRIZZLY BEAR CAN SNIFF OUT FOOD 18 MILES (29 km) AWAY.

HELLO, HOW ARE YOU TODAY?
WHITE-FACED
CAPUCHIN MONKEYS
GREET EACH OTHER BY
STICKING THEIR
FINGERS UP EACH OTHER'S NOSE.

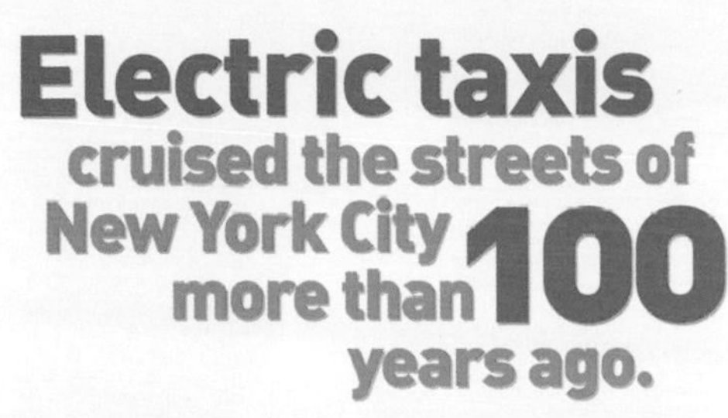

Electric taxis cruised the streets of New York City more than 100 years ago.

New Zealand has more cats per person than any other country in the world.

A JAPANESE ARTIST MAKES SHELLS FOR HERMIT CRABS THAT LOOK LIKE CITY SKYLINES.

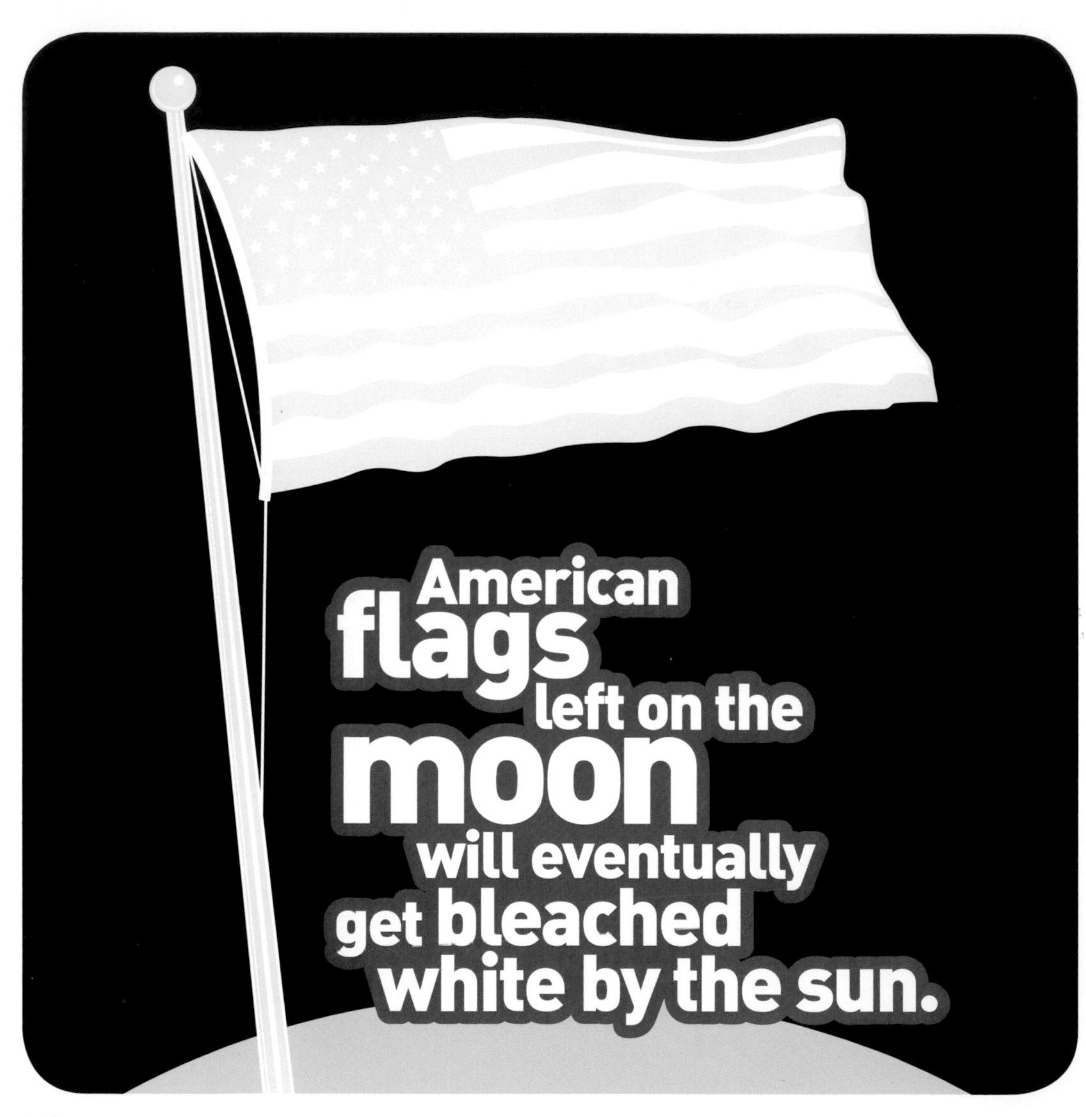
American
flags
left on the
moon
will eventually
get bleached
white by the sun.

A designer created a glow-in-the-dark wedding dress.

Boomerang
K99

AN **ICE-CREAM TRUCK** IN LONDON SERVED **SCOOPS** JUST FOR **DOGS.**

IT DOESN'T RAIN IN THE EYE OF A HURRICANE.

It is impossible to **hum** while holding your nose.

Atlantic lobsters sometimes **eat** each other.

A PICTURE PAINTED BY A RETIRED RACEHORSE SOLD FOR MORE THAN $2,000 ON eBAY.

A PALM TREE is not a tree; it's a type of GRASS.

NASCAR DRIVERS CAN TRAVEL THE LENGTH

OF A **FOOTBALL FIELD** IN JUST OVER A **SECOND.**

Some early baseballs were made of fish eyes covered in leather.

An ELEPHANT'S skin is as thick as 12 stacked PENNIES.

A STUDY FOUND THAT CHEESE MAY TASTE SALTIER IF YOU EAT IT OFF A KNIFE INSTEAD OF A FORK.

STICK TO A FORK. IT'S SAFER!

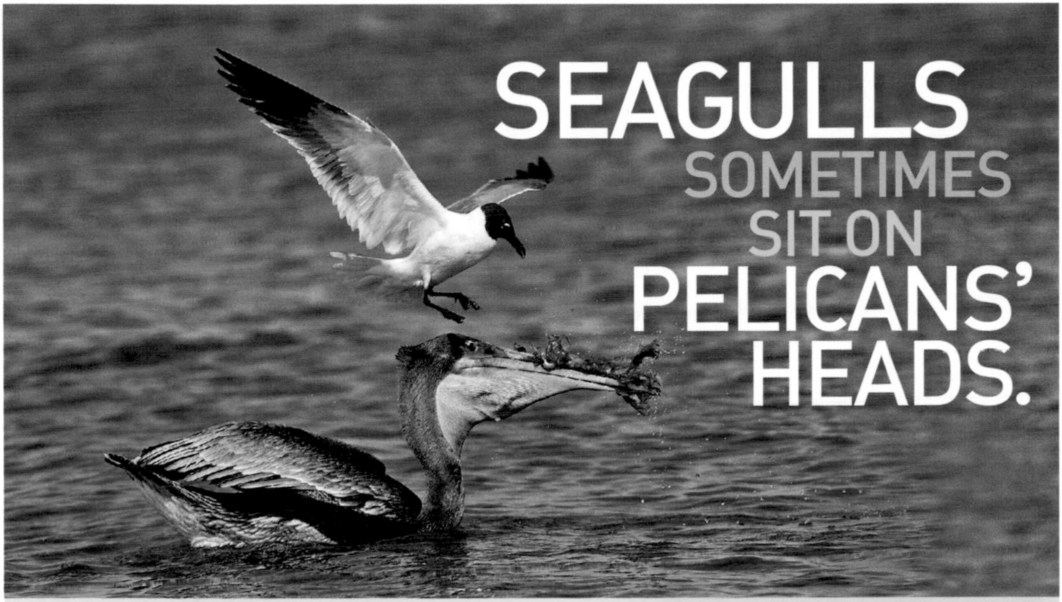

SEAGULLS SOMETIMES SIT ON PELICANS' HEADS.

The White House, in Washington, D.C., U.S.A.,

was originally called the **President's Palace.**

A luxury **hotel** distributes 24-karat-gold **iPads** to its guests in Dubai, United Arab Emirates.

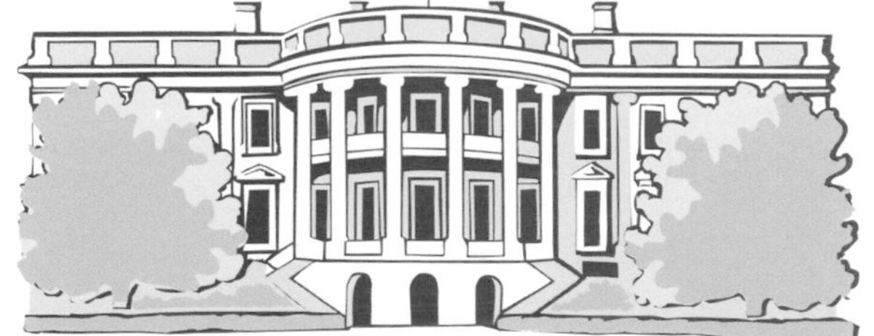

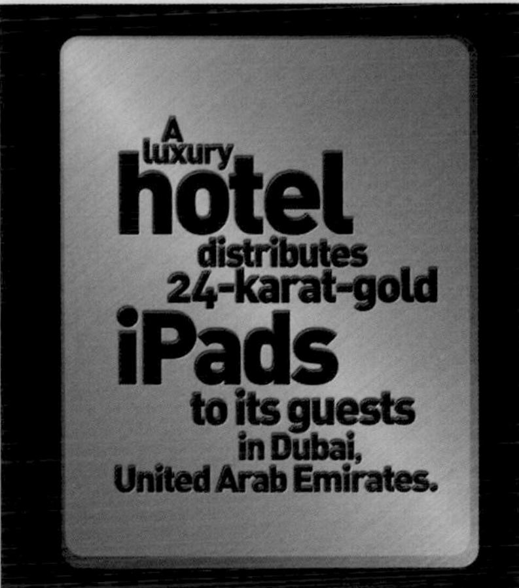

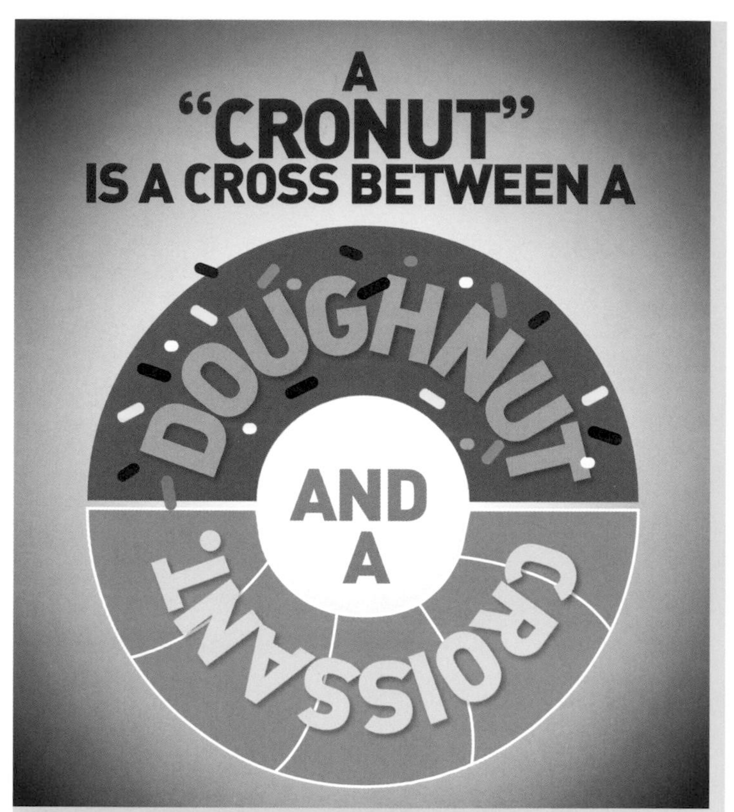

Amazon.com was originally called **"CADABRA."**

CHIMPANZEES CAN SWIM THE *BREASTSTROKE.*

AN EMU'S BODY CONTAINS UP TO THREE GALLONS (11.4 L) OF OIL— ENOUGH TO FILL THREE MILK JUGS.

1,360 OLYMPIC-SIZE SWIMMING POOLS COULD FIT

INTO THE **WORLD'S LARGEST BUILDING**, LOCATED IN CHINA.

YOU LOSE ABOUT A **MILLION SKIN CELLS** EVERY **24 HOURS.**

The first-ever webcam was used to watch a pot of coffee.

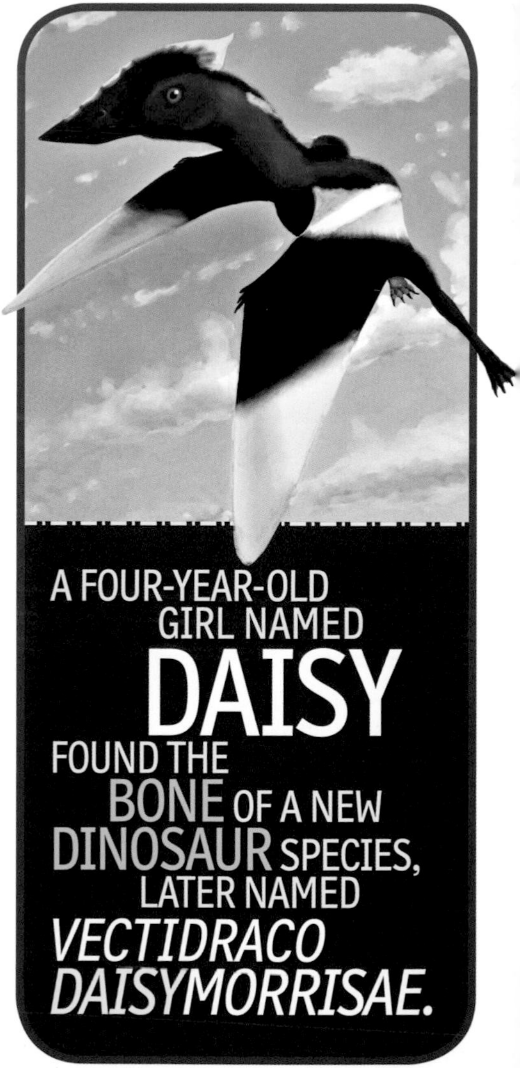

A FOUR-YEAR-OLD GIRL NAMED **DAISY** FOUND THE BONE OF A NEW DINOSAUR SPECIES, LATER NAMED *VECTIDRACO DAISYMORRISAE.*

Nosewise, Sturdy, and Hardy were popular names for dogs in medieval times.

SOME MOTHS' HEARING IS 15 TIMES MORE SENSITIVE THAN A HUMAN'S.

Muscles make up about **half** your body weight.

The **COOKIECUTTER SHARK** is named for the **COOKIE-SHAPED WOUNDS** it leaves in its **PREY.**

YOU CAN BUY **CANDY** THAT YOU CAN DRINK FROM A MINI– **TOILET BOWL.**

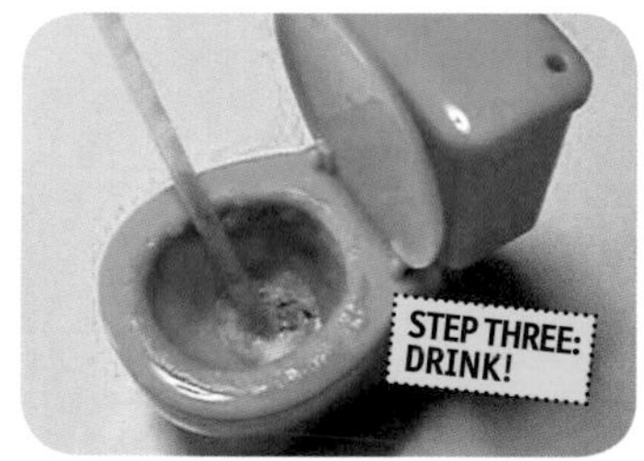

Giant kelp can grow up to two feet in a day. (0.6 m)

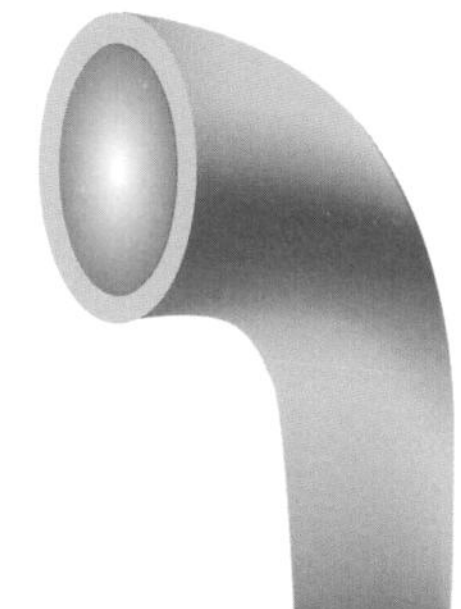

You can get a massage 20 feet (6 m) under the sea in the world's first submarine spa.

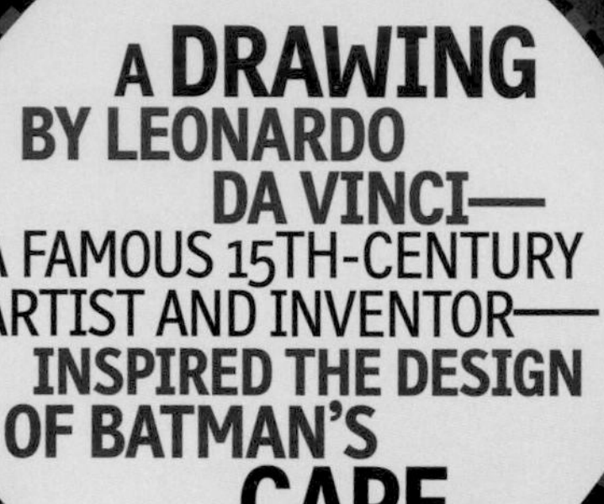

A DRAWING BY LEONARDO DA VINCI—A FAMOUS 15TH-CENTURY ARTIST AND INVENTOR—INSPIRED THE DESIGN OF BATMAN'S CAPE.

MUSICIANS RE-CREATED THE BATMAN THEME SONG USING REAL BAT SOUNDS.

THERE'S AN AIRPORT IN TURKEY NAMED BATMAN.

THE ORIGINAL **BATMOBILE** FROM THE 1960s *BATMAN* TV SHOW SOLD FOR **$4.2 MILLION.**

SOME FISH
USE THEIR FINS
TO WALK
ALONG THE
OCEAN FLOOR.

The world's biggest passenger jet weighs as much as 100 hippos.

Pac-Man's
shape was
inspired by
a whole
with a
slice
removed.

BALD PEOPLE ACTUALLY HAVE MICROSCOPIC HAIRS ON THEIR HEADS.

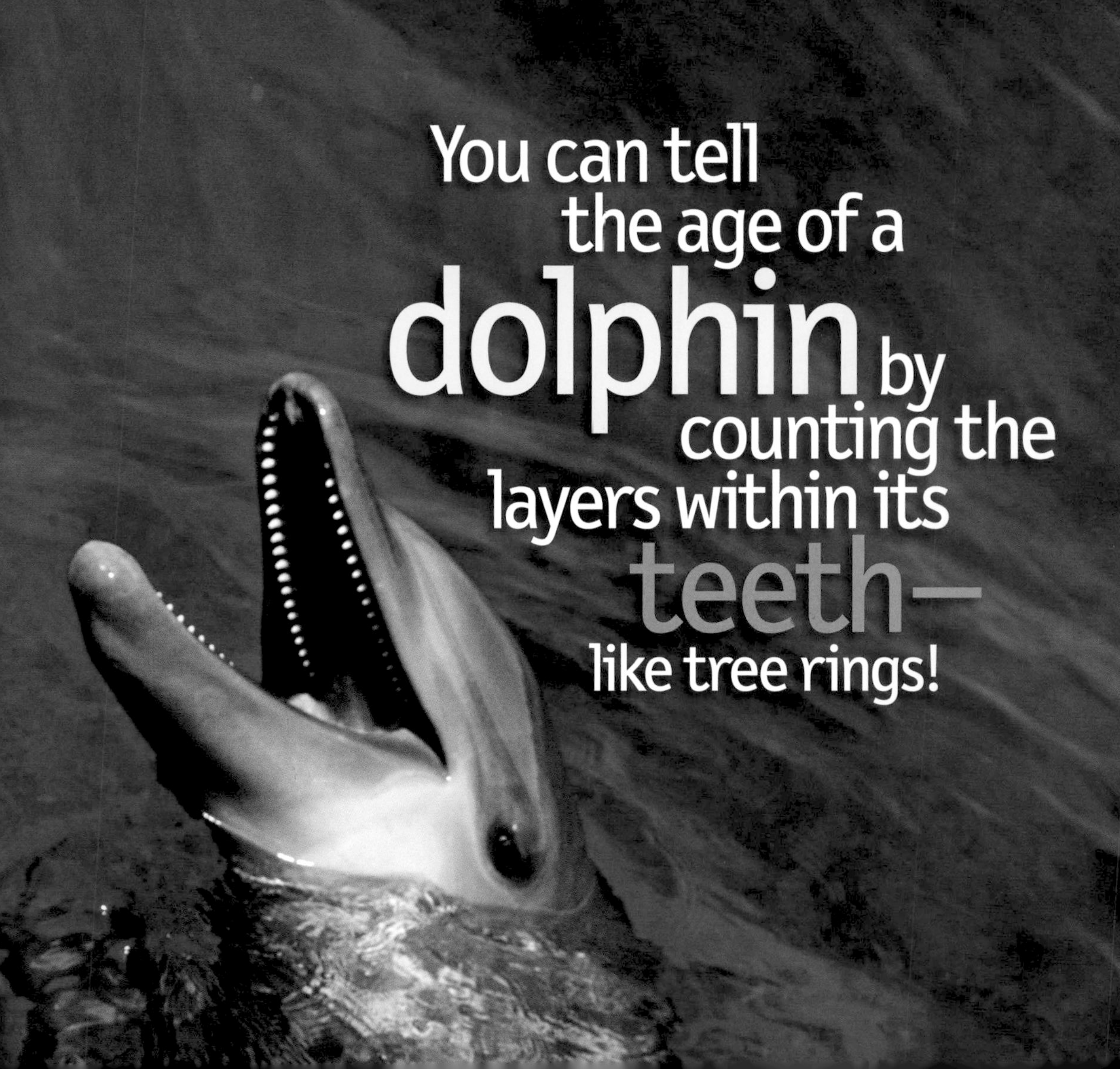
You can tell
the age of a
dolphin by
counting the
layers within its
teeth—
like tree rings!

DOLPHINS CAN RECOGNIZE AN OLD FRIEND'S WHISTLE,
EVEN AFTER THEY'VE BEEN SEPARATED FOR 20 YEARS.

Rabbits can see behind them without moving their heads.

THERE'S A MONUMENT DEDICATED TO THE BOLL WEEVIL BUG IN ALABAMA, U.S.A.

AILUROPHOBIA IS AN EXTREME FEAR OF CATS.

Geckos communicate by barking, chirping, and squeaking.

Shrimp swim BACKWARD.

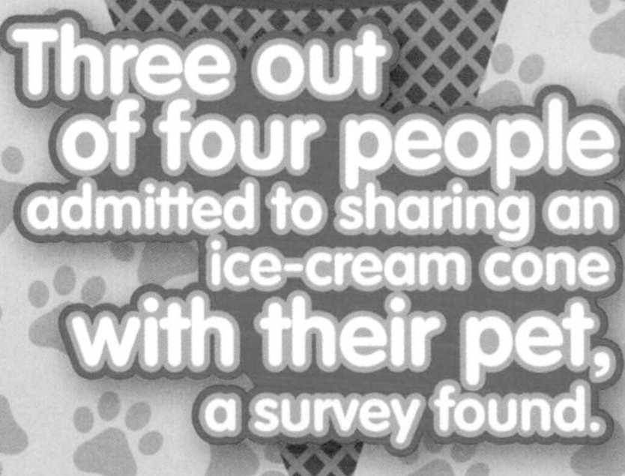

Three out of four people admitted to sharing an ice-cream cone with their pet, a survey found.

Flatworms can **regrow** their heads.

More than **200 million emails** are sent **every minute** *on Earth.*

A PRISON IN BRAZIL USES GEESE AS AN ALARM SYSTEM—THEY HONK AT ANYONE ROAMING THE GROUNDS!

STOP WHERE YOU ARE!

THE MIMIC OCTOPUS CAN CHANGE SHAPE TO LOOK LIKE OTHER ANIMALS.
SEA SNAKE?
MANTIS SHRIMP?
FLOUNDER?

HUNDREDS OF YEARS AGO,
RUSSIANS
BUILT THE FIRST
ROLLER COASTERS
FROM **ICE.**

There's a **frog** that hears through its **mouth.**

THAT'S WEIRD!

CORN FLAKES CEREAL was first served in a hospital as an easy-to-digest food.

You have taste buds in your throat.

A woman once made a whoopie pie weighing 1,062 pounds (482 kg)—enough for 6,000 servings.

BAKED CATERPILLARS TASTE LIKE PISTACHIOS.

DON'T TRY THIS AT HOME!

The **blue whale**—the largest animal on Earth—**can't swallow anything bigger than a beach ball.**

BLUE WHALE CALVES GAIN 9 POUNDS (4 kg) PER HOUR

BLUE WHALES DO UNDERWATER BARREL ROLLS BEFORE **CATCHING PREY.**

FOR THE FIRST SEVEN MONTHS OF THEIR LIVES,

STUDIES SHOW THAT THE
IS ABOUT
14 SECONDS
LONG.

Male
pandas
sometimes
do handstands
to mark
trees.

For $25, you can order a jar of human toenails online.

THE SPEED OF LIGHT IS 18 MILLION TIMES FASTER THAN THE SPEED OF RAIN.

The *Kilauea volcano* on the Big Island of Hawaii, U.SA., has been erupting for 30 years.

Before it hit stores, the iPhone was known as "Purple."

SOME BIRDS HIBERNATE.

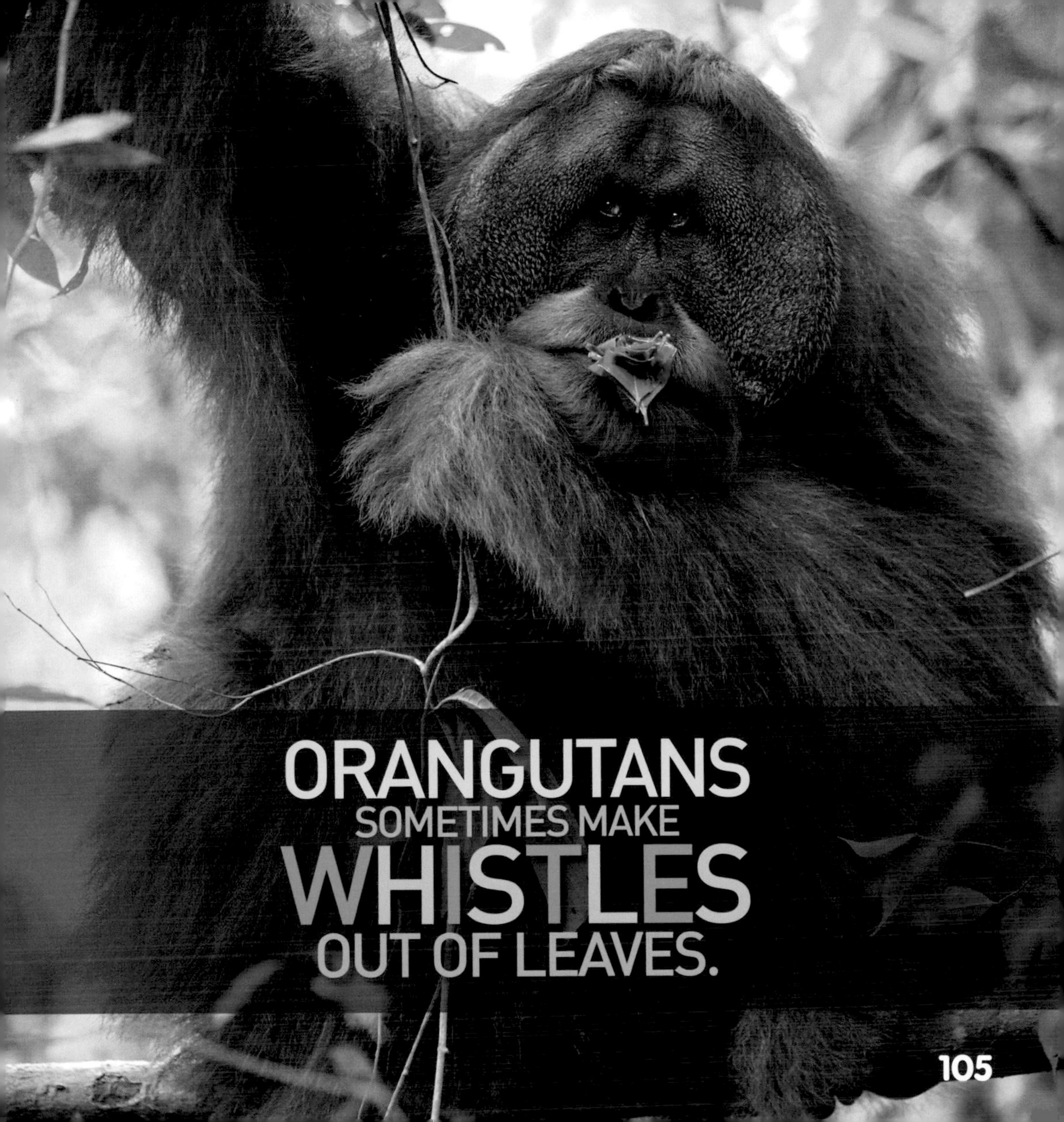
ORANGUTANS
SOMETIMES MAKE
WHISTLES
OUT OF LEAVES.

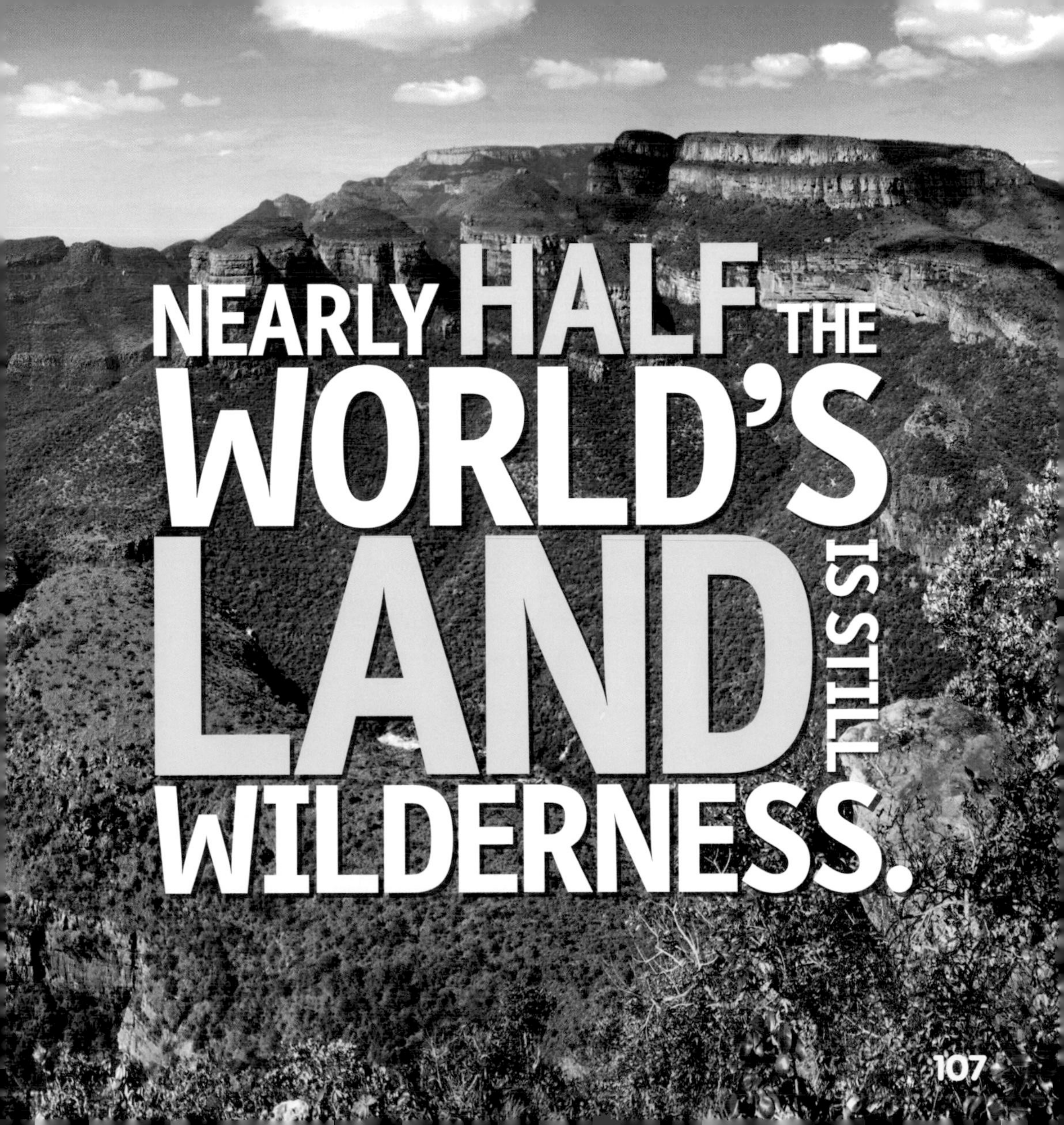

NEARLY HALF THE WORLD'S LAND IS STILL WILDERNESS.

100 billion
servings of
instant
ramen
noodles
are
sold every year.
(That's 14 bowls for every
person on Earth!)

EVERY YEAR, RESIDENTS IN A NEW MEXICO, U.S.A., TOWN BUILD A **GIANT SNOWMAN** OUT OF **TUMBLEWEEDS.**

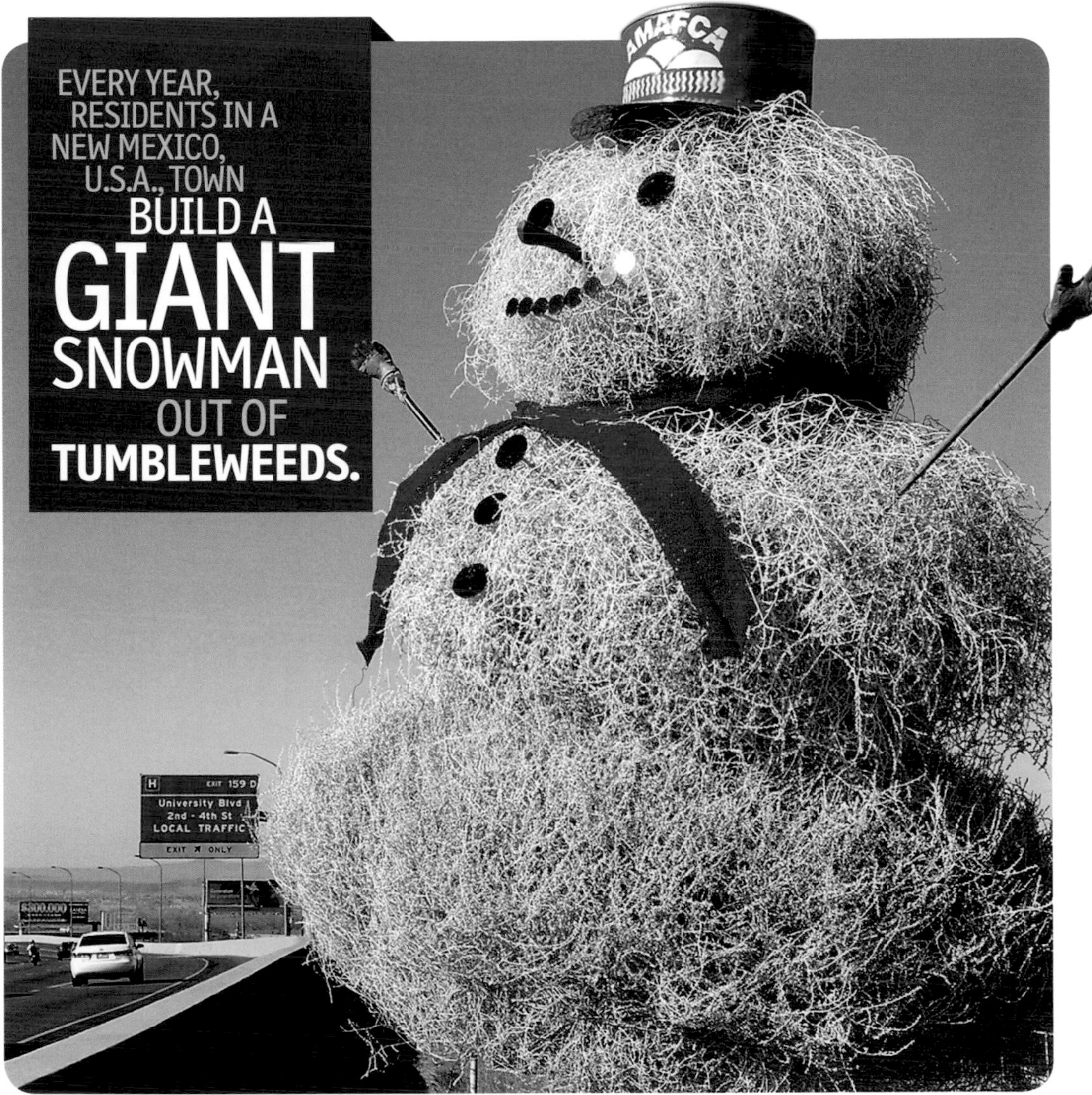

The longest unbroken apple peel was as long as an Olympic-size pool.

A restaurant in Singapore once sold a pizza within a pizza.

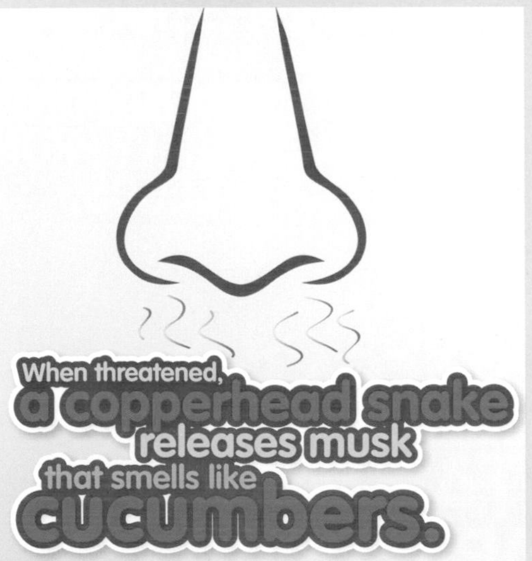

STORM SYSTEMS IN THE SKY CAN HOLD MORE WATER THAN THE MISSISSIPPI RIVER.

IT TOOK **ARTISTS** SOME 17,000 **HOURS** TO BUILD A **LIFE-SIZE STAR WARS X-WING STARFIGHTER** ENTIRELY FROM **LEGOS.**

THE FURRY CHEWBACCA BAT IS NAMED AFTER THE STAR WARS CHARACTER.

A FAST FOOD RESTAURANT IN FRANCE OFFERS DARTH VADER BURGERS WITH BUNS THAT ARE DYED BLACK.

IT WOULD TAKE 225 MILLION YEARS TO WALK A LIGHT-YEAR.

You can order deep-fried jelly beans at some state fairs.

There are only two sets of escalators in the entire state of Wyoming, U.S.A.

A ROBOT OFFICIATED A WEDDING IN JAPAN.

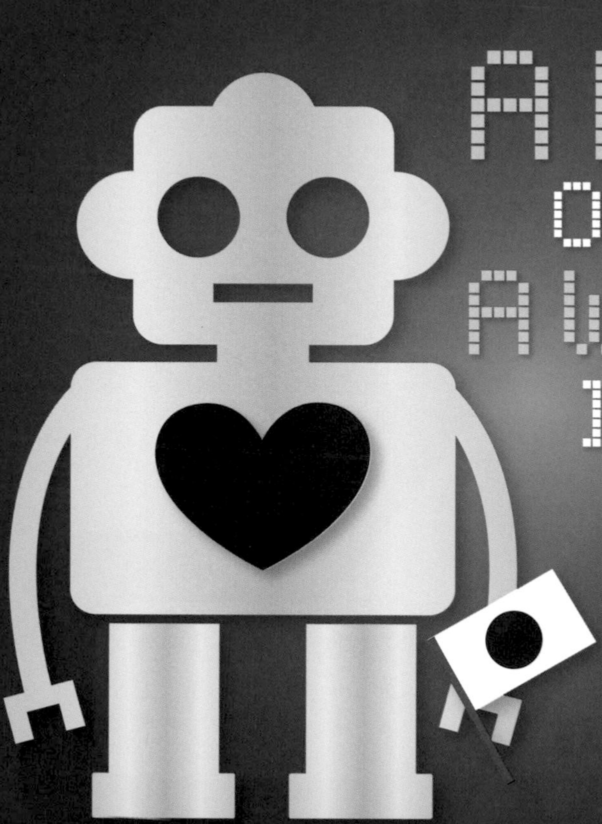

Redheads in Australia are sometimes called "Blueys."

The meteorite that most likely killed off the dinosaurs was the size of San Francisco, California, U.S.A.

Donald Duck's middle name is FAUNTLEROY.

THE OARFISH CAN GROW TO BE LONGER THAN A SCHOOL BUS.

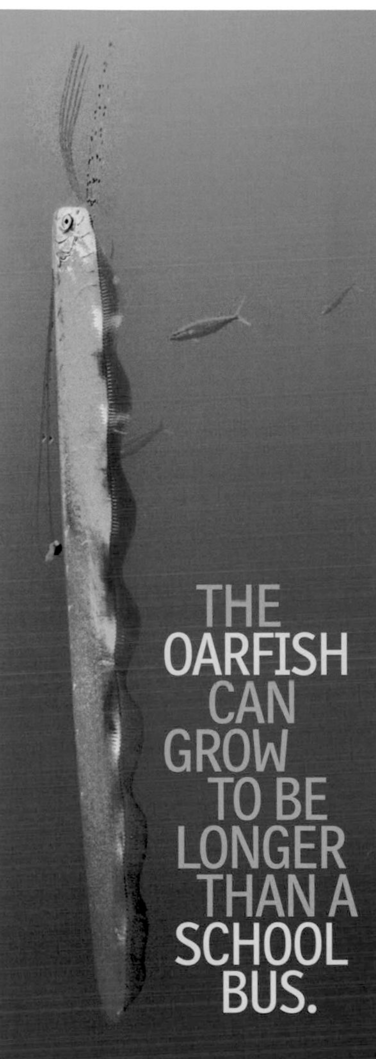

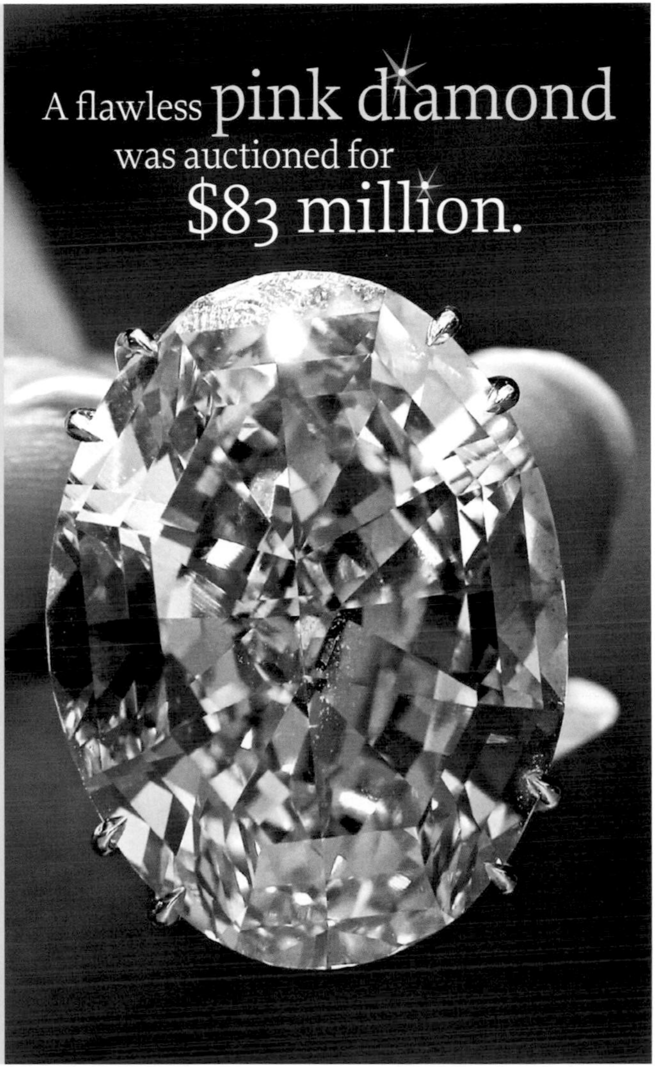

A flawless pink diamond was auctioned for $83 million.

SOME ZOO ANIMALS SNACK ON **"BLOODSICLES"** TO STAY COOL DURING HEAT WAVES.

Choir members' heartbeats sync when they sing, a study found.

AN AUSTRIAN PHOTOGRAPHER TURNED A SHIPWRECK INTO AN UNDERWATER ART GALLERY.

A ZOO in England banned visitors from wearing animal print clothes to avoid confusing the wildlife.

IT TAKES ABOUT
THE SAME AMOUNT OF
force
TO PULL YOUR FOOT
OUT OF
quicksand
AS IT DOES TO
lift a car.

Soccer's World Cup trophy is worth about $250,000!

There's a **world snail racing championship** held in England every year.

THE LION'S MANE JELLYFISH CAN GROW TO BE LONGER THAN SEVEN SUVs.

THE CITY OF
AMSTERDAM,
IN THE NETHERLANDS,
HAS MORE
BIKES
THAN PEOPLE.

CATS AND DOGS CAN GET SUNBURNED.

In Belgium, there are postage stamps that smell and taste like chocolate.

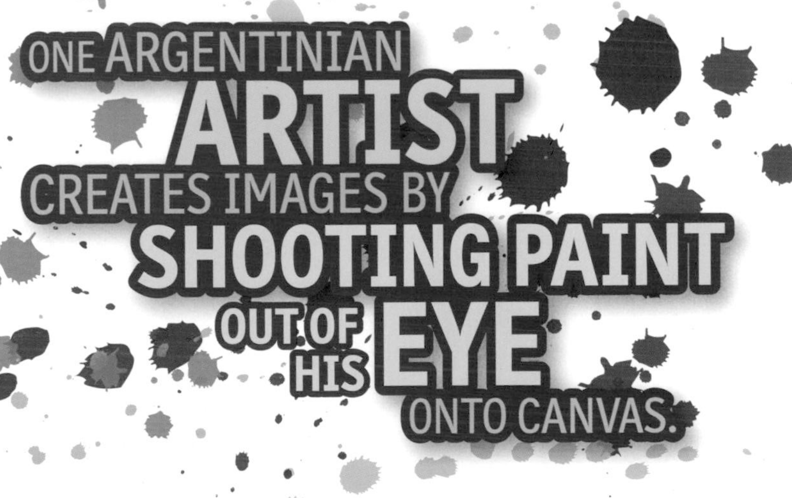

ONE ARGENTINIAN ARTIST CREATES IMAGES BY SHOOTING PAINT OUT OF HIS EYE ONTO CANVAS.

SOME LIZARDS HAVE GREEN BONES.

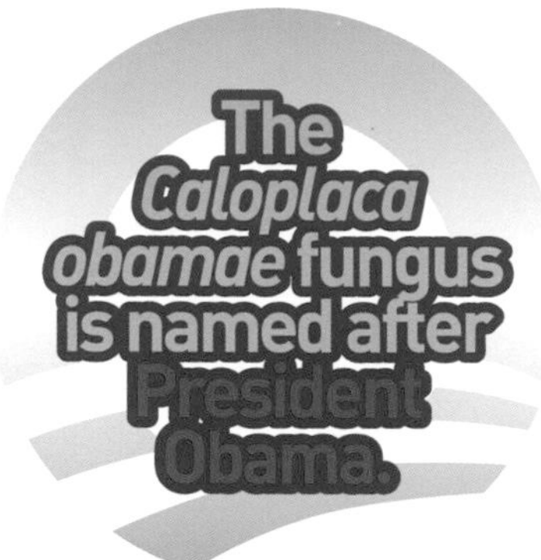

People tend to
sleep less
when there's a
FULL MOON.

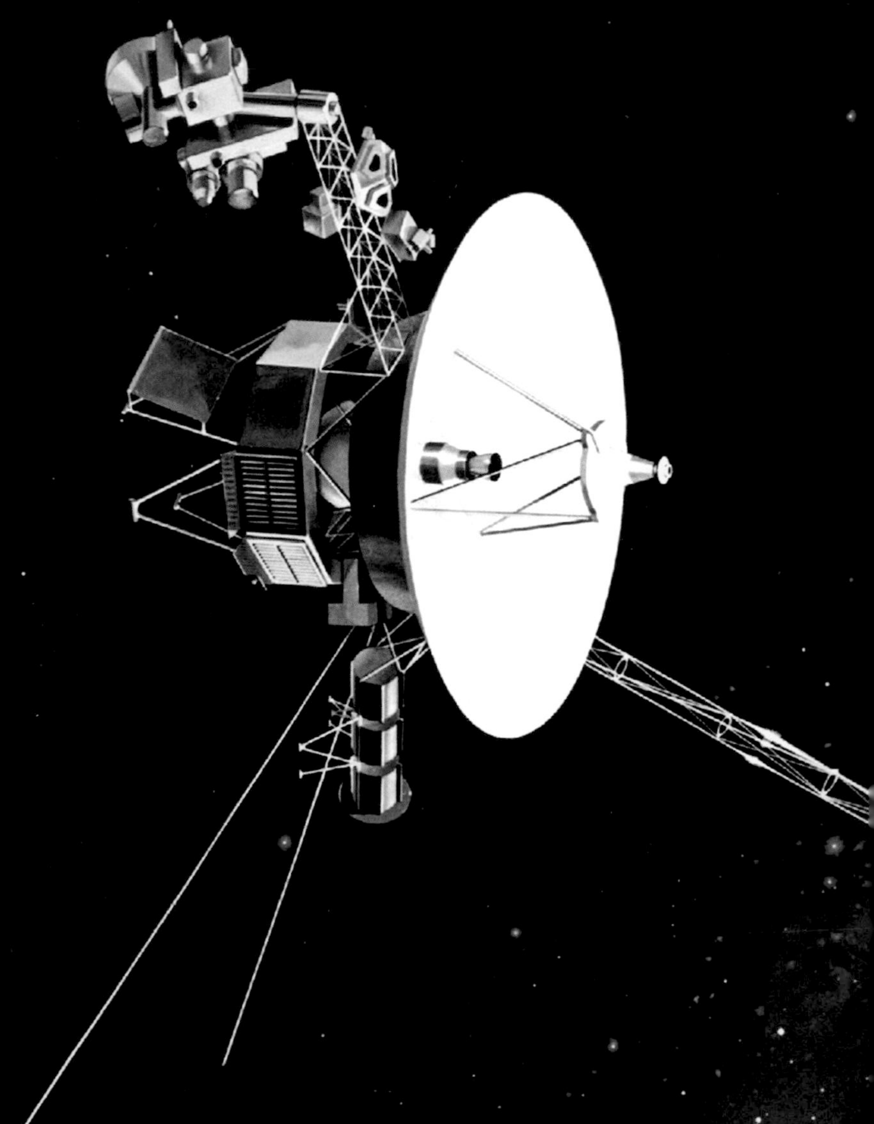

Voyager 1 is the first spacecraft to leave the solar system—more than 11 billion miles (17,702,784,000 km) from Earth.

A MANHATTAN **PIZZERIA** SELLS A **12-INCH** (31-cm) **PIZZA** WITH CAVIAR TOPPING FOR **$1,000.**

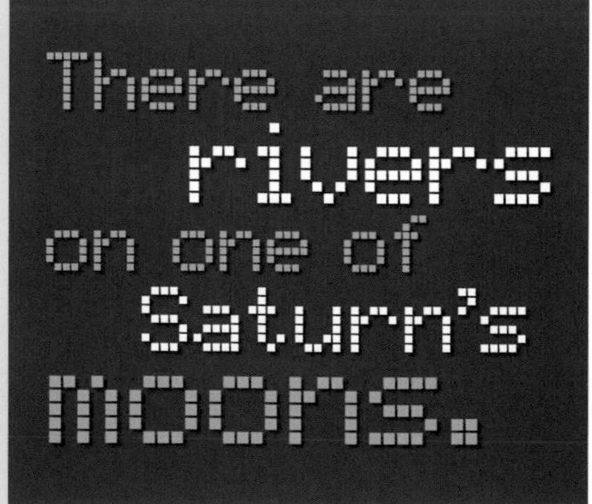

SOME
RATS
ARE TRAINED TO
SNIFF OUT
BOMBS.

You can buy
cola-flavored
Cheetos
in Japan.

About half the people ON EARTH live in an area where SNOW never falls.

Parrotfish sleep in a bag of their own mucus.

THAT'S COZY!

RAINBOW
EUCALYPTUS TREES
HAVE MULTICOLORED BARK.

A tiny park in Oregon, U.S.A., is smaller than a skateboard.

A WOMAN IN FLORIDA, U.S.A., FOUND A **STRAWBERRY** SHAPED LIKE A GRIZZLY BEAR.

There's a machine that turns sweat into drinking water.

The first Tweet from Google read "I'm 01100110 01100101 01100101 01101100 01101001 01101110 01100111 00100000 01101100 01110101 01100011 01101011 01111001 00001010."

SCOOBY-DOO WAS ORIGINALLY NAMED TOO MUCH.

TIGERS AND HOUSE CATS

SHARE 95 PERCENT OF THE SAME GENES.

Northern Spy,
Wealthy, and
Twenty Ounce
are all types of
apples.

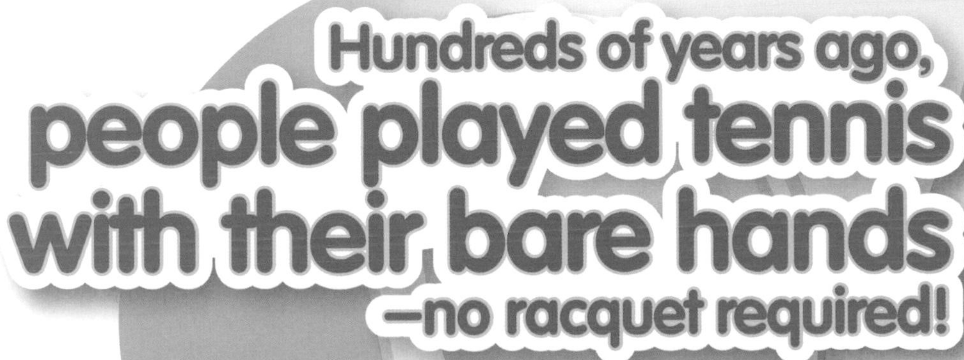

Hundreds of years ago,
people played tennis with their bare hands
–no racquet required!

King cobras
can grow
as long as a
giraffe
is tall.

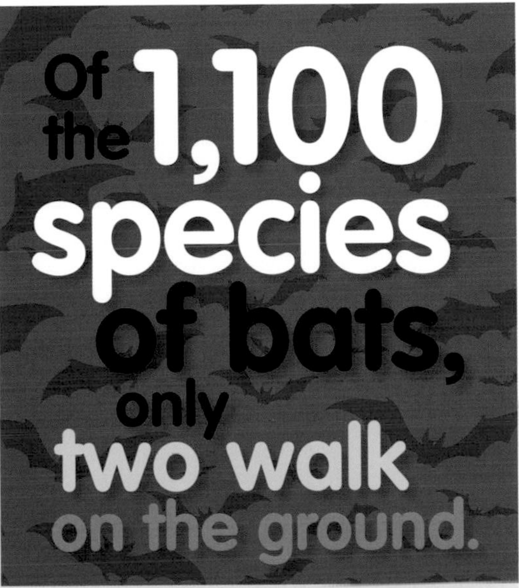

AN EXTINCT
VOLCANO
THE SIZE OF
ITALY LIES
UNDERNEATH THE
PACIFIC OCEAN.

CHIHUAHUA
DACHSHUND

CHIWEENIE

SOME **FISH** CAN **GROW** ALMOST A **QUARTER OF THEIR BODY LENGTH** IN A SINGLE DAY.

Earth bulges at the Equator.

It would take the strength of five people to "tip" a standing cow.

HELLO
my name is
THE BIRD ON THE TWITTER LOGO IS NAMED LARRY.

SCOLIONOPHOBIA IS A FEAR OF SCHOOL.

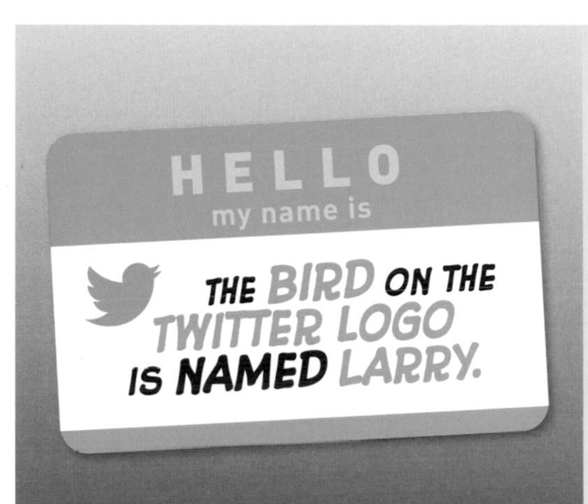

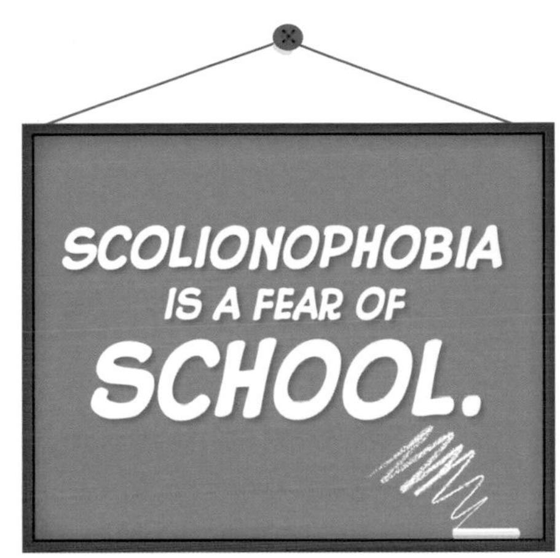

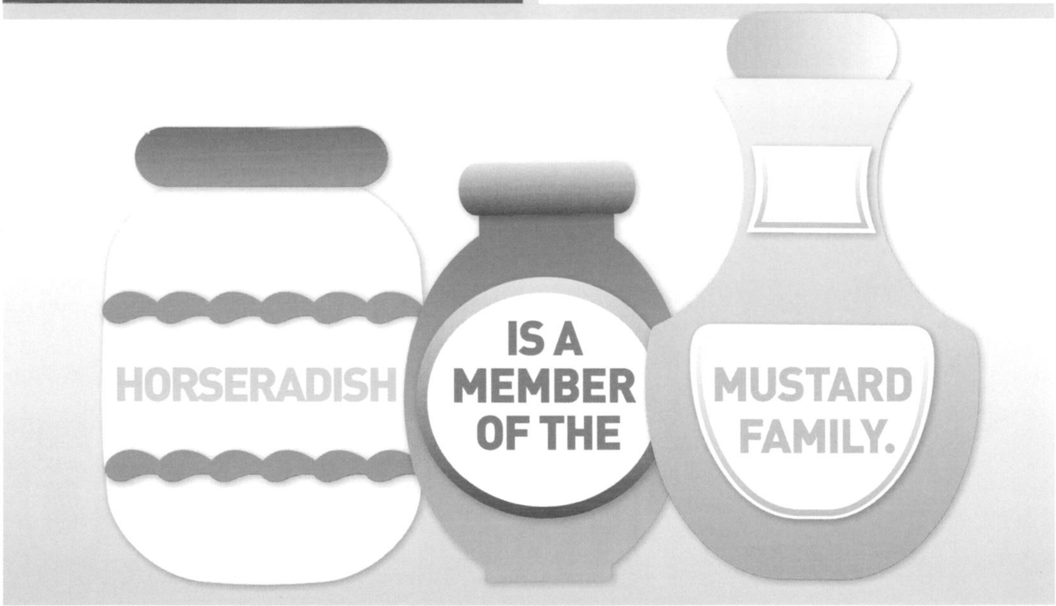
HORSERADISH
IS A MEMBER OF THE
MUSTARD FAMILY.

SEVERAL SHIPS ARE BURIED

UNDER BUILDINGS

IN SAN FRANCISCO, CALIFORNIA, U.S.A.

PEOPLE WAITED IN A 7-MILE (11 km) LINE TO EAT AT THE FIRST-EVER MCDONALD'S IN KUWAIT.

Today's
cell phones
are more
POWERFUL
than the computers
that sent
ASTRONAUTS
to the
MOON.

Alaska
is the
northernmost,
westernmost,
and easternmost
state in the
United States.

AVOCADOS
ARE TOXIC
TO MOST
BIRDS.

THE SHORTEST COMMERCIAL FLIGHT
IS JUST TWO MINUTES LONG.

"Watermelon snow" IS TINTED PINK AND SMELLS SWEET.

SOME BUTTERFLIES DRINK TURTLE TEARS.

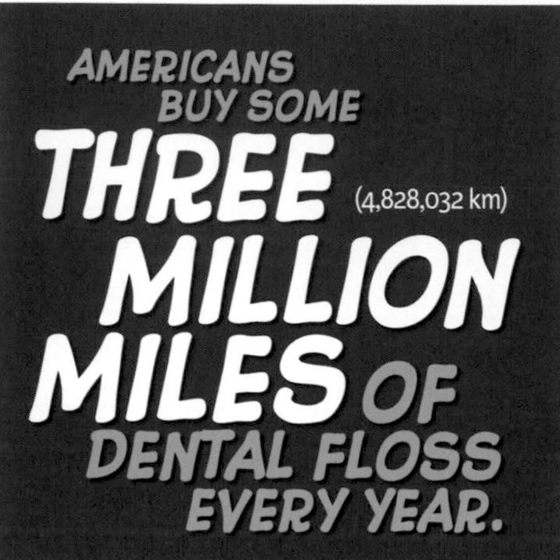

Vinegar can dissolve pearls.

WHEN THREATENED, THE HELLBENDER SALAMANDER, ALSO CALLED A SNOT OTTER, OOZES CLEAR SLIME.

Gorillas sleep in nests.

You spend about an hour a day CHEWING.

ALL CLOWNFISH ARE BORN MALE.

THE EYE OF A HURRICANE ON SATURN IS SO HUGE, IT WOULD STRETCH FROM LONDON, ENGLAND, TO MOSCOW, RUSSIA.

Thousands of brand-new **sneakers** once washed ashore on a **Dutch island.**

Some astronauts train for space walks by walking on the OCEAN FLOOR.

Giant CLAMS
can grow
AS LONG AS two
skateboards.

Kiwifruits were originally called "melonettes."

A MAN FLOATED
FOR
235 MILES
(378 km)
IN A
CHAIR
TIED TO
MORE THAN
150
HELIUM
BALLOONS.

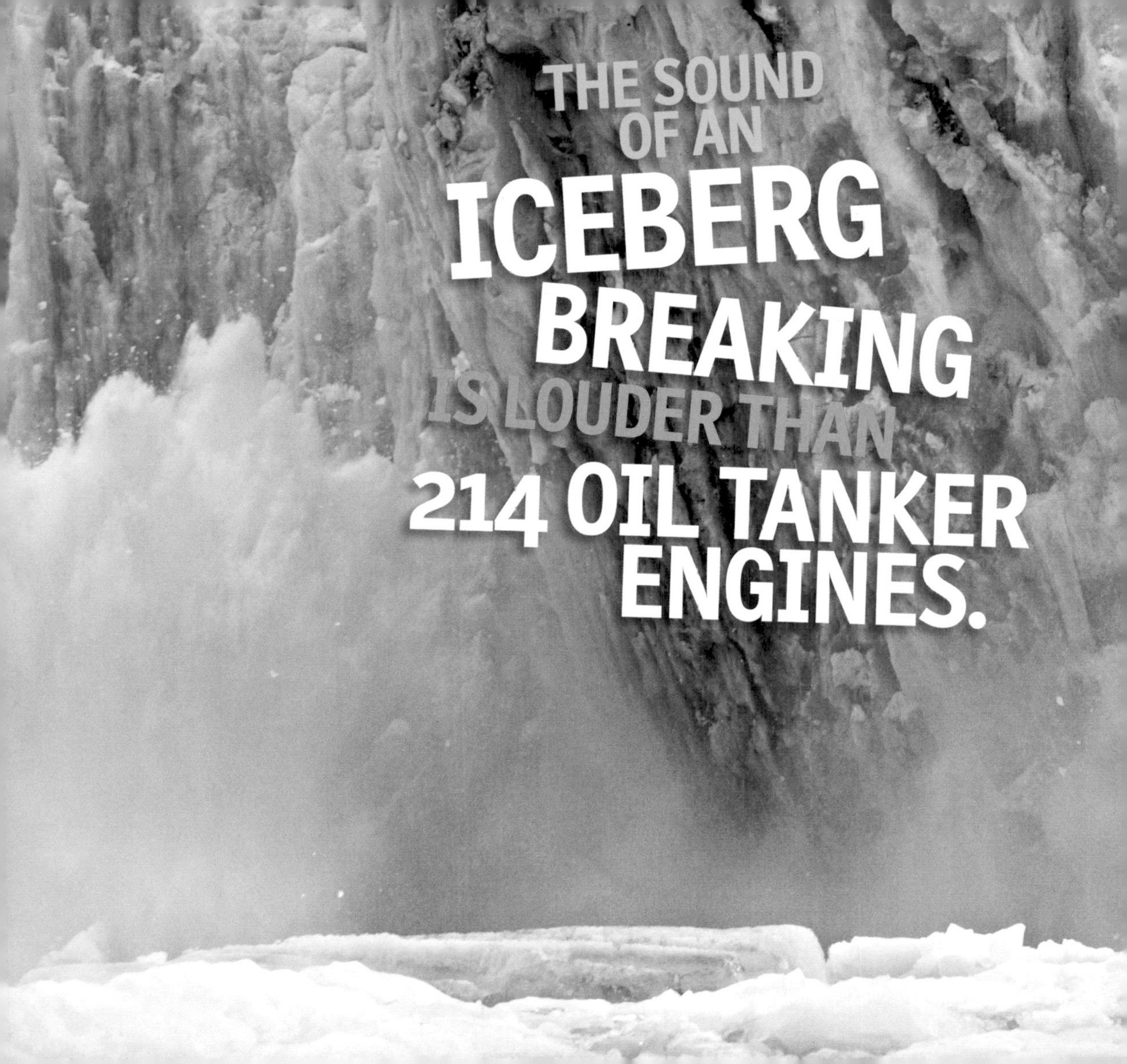

THE SOUND
OF AN
ICEBERG
BREAKING
IS LOUDER THAN
214 OIL TANKER
ENGINES.

A FISHERMAN NEAR NORWAY REELED IN A 9-FOOT-LONG (2.7-m) HALIBUT THAT WEIGHED MORE THAN A GORILLA.

PIGEONS CAN RECOGNIZE THEMSELVES IN A MIRROR.

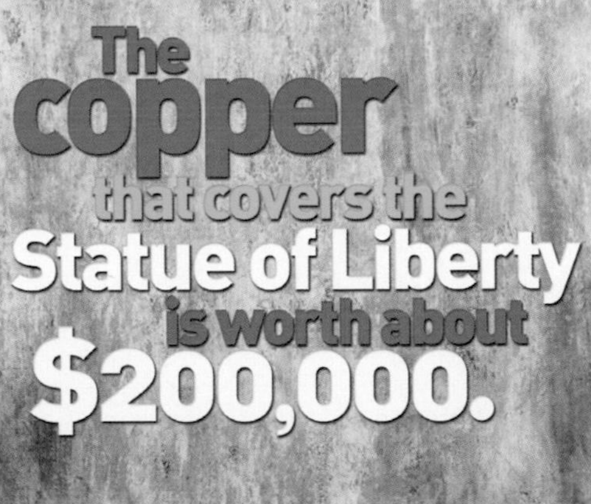

A whale's **EARWAX** can be as thick as a **mattress.**

You can stay IN A luxury cave at an inn in NEW MEXICO, U.S.A.

SCIENTISTS THINK THAT IT RAINS GLASS ON SOME PLANETS.

THERE ARE NO SEAGULLS IN HAWAII, U.S.A.

ASH FROM VOLCANIC ERUPTIONS CAN MAKE THE MOON LOOK BLUE FROM EARTH.

Snub-nosed monkeys sneeze when it rains.

TURKEY LEGS
SMOKED

EIGHT COLLEGE FOOTBALL PLAYERS COMPETED AGAINST TWO ASIAN ELEPHANTS IN A WATERMELON-EATING CONTEST.

(THE HUMANS LOST.)

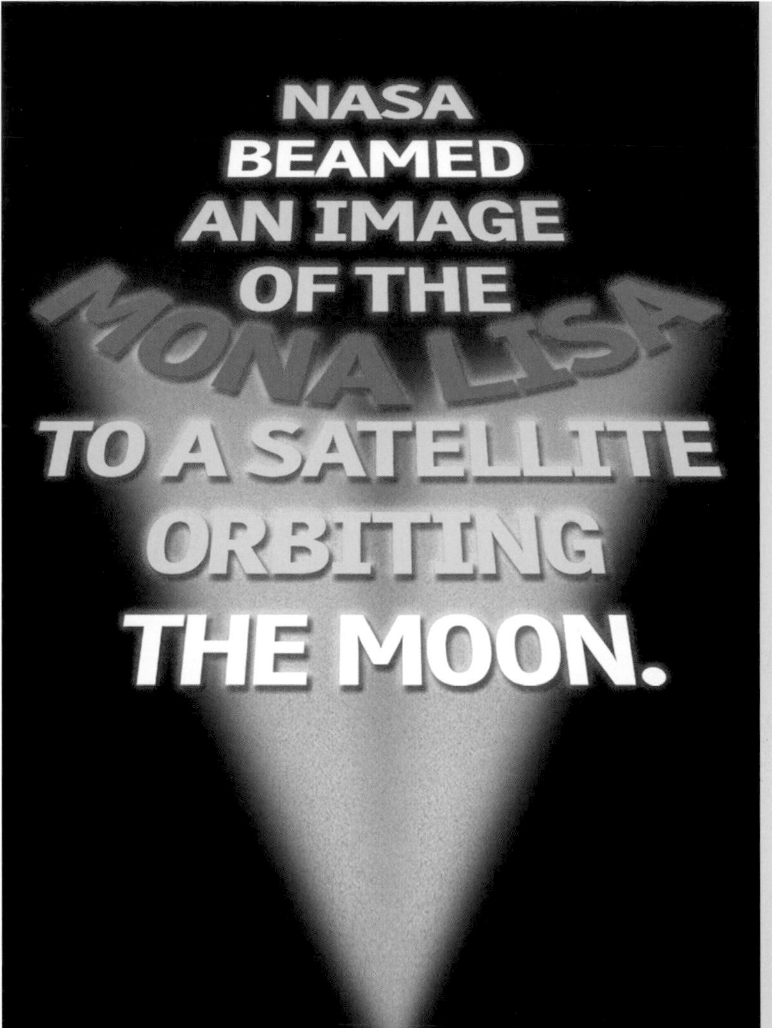

PREHISTORIC PEOPLE USED "SUPERGLUE" MADE FROM **TREE SAP** AND PIGMENT **SOME 70,000 YEARS AGO.**

THERE ARE ABOUT 300 DIMPLES ON A GOLF BALL.

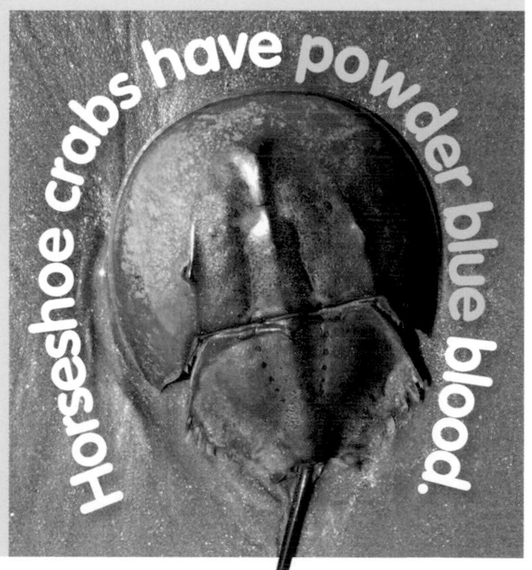

THE THINNEST GLASS IN THE WORLD IS 20-BILLIONTHS OF AN INCH (2.5 CM) THICK.

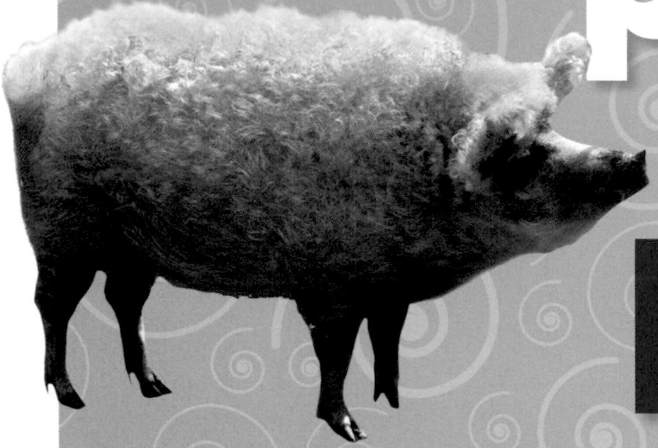

Some pigs have curly hair.

Music broadcast from the International Space Station played over the radio on Earth.

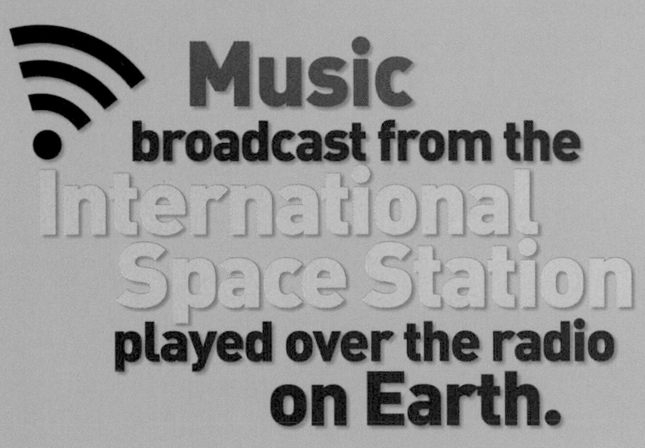

SOME MOTH COCOONS CAN BE USED TO MAKE PURSES.

SOME FISH CAN TASTE WITH THEIR TAILS.

The scientific name for brain freeze is *sphenopalatine ganglioneuralgia.*

CHIPMUNKS see in *slow motion.*

Tyrannosaurus Rex could probably swim.

THERE'S A HOTEL WITH GUEST ROOMS MADE OUT OF OLD DRAINAGE PIPES.

Large crocodiles can survive for more than a year without eating.

THERE ARE
MORE THAN
1,900
EDIBLE
INSECT SPECIES
ON EARTH.

THERE'S A BAND THAT PLAYS INSTRUMENTS MADE FROM OLD CAR PARTS.

THE "STRUTBONE" IS MADE FROM THE STRUTS OF A CAR!

Flying vampire frogs have black fangs when they are tadpoles.

Lipstick-wearers who lick their lips can eat up to two spoonfuls of makeup a year.

YOU HAVE ABOUT FOUR MILLION SWEAT GLANDS IN YOUR BODY.

There's a pink lake in Australia.

A NEW TYPE OF WETSUIT CAMOUFLAGES

SURFERS SO SHARKS CAN'T SEE THEM.

Scientists think sharks are color-blind.

FACTFINDER

Illustrations are indicated by **boldface.**

PHOTO CREDITS

Cover: (pig), Tsekhmister/iStockphoto; Spine: Tsekhmister/Shutterstock; 2, Tsekhmister/Shutterstock; 4-5, iStockphoto; 6, Wan Norazalini Wan Hassan/Shutterstock; 8, Xavier Eichaker/Biosphoto; 9, Wikimedia Commons; 10-11, Lisa & Mike Husar/TeamHusar.com; 13, beboy/Shutterstock; 14, courtesy of Robert Wood, Wyss Institute for Biologically Inspired Engineering, Harvard University; 15 (bottom, left), Ilya Akinshin/Shutterstock; 15 (right), Wikimedia Commons; 16-17, Tui De Roy/Minden Pictures; 19, WENN.com/Newscom; 21, Wikimedia Commons; 22, Annette Shaff/Shutterstock; 23, Eric Isselée/Shutterstock; 25, SuperStock; 26, M & Y News Ltd/Rex USA; 28-29, Anton Foltin/Shutterstock; 31, Alex Wild/Visuals Unlimited, Inc.; 32, iStockphoto; 33, Natural Visions/Alamy; 34-35, Krzysztof Wiktor/Shutterstock; 37, WENN.com/Newscom; 38 (left), courtesy Jantina Wennerstrom; 38 (right), Sergy64/Shutterstock; 39, courtesy of Shuhai Xiao; 40-41, Shigeru Ban by Didier Boy de la Tour Photographe; 42, Bernhard Seifert, Senckenberg Museum of Natural History; 43 (top left, background), iStockphoto; 43 (top left, front), s oleg/Shutterstock; 44, AFP/Getty Images; 46, EuroPics/Newscom; 48, Richard Figueiredo/WENN.com/Newscom; 49, Henk Verbiesen/Biosphoto; 52 (left), Four Oaks/Shutterstock; 52 (right), Mayovskyy Andrew/Shutterstock; 52-53 (background), Pakhnyushcha/Shutterstock; 56 (left), courtesy of Paper Pulp Helmet; 56 (top, right), Aaron Amat/Shutterstock, 56 (bottom, right), Bonnie Taylor Barry/Shutterstock; 57, Mehau Kulyk/Science Source; 58 (left), Denis Tabler/Shutterstock; 58-59, Patricio Robles Gil/Sierra Madre/Minden Pictures; 58 (right), Potapov Alexander/Shutterstock; 60, Pat Canova/Alamy; 61, Aki Inomata, courtesy of Ai Kowada Gallery, Tokyo; 63, courtesy Designer Loft Productions; 64, Solent News/Splash News/Newscom; 65, WilleeCole/Shutterstock; 66, NASA; 68, Wendy Wooley; 70-71, Beelde Photography/Shutterstock; 72 (left), absolut/Shutterstock; 72 (top, right), iStockphoto; 72 (bottom, right), Ljupco Smokovski/iStockphoto; 73, Sylvain Cordier/Biosphoto; 75, iStockphoto; 76, AFP/Getty Images/Newscom; 78, Isle of Wight County Pre/REX USA; 79 (left), Robynrg/Shutterstock; 79 (center), Vladyslav Starozhylov/Shutterstock; 79 (right), Jagodka/Shutterstock; 80 (top), courtesy youtube/RRcherrypie; 80 (center), courtesy youtube/RRcherrypie; 80 (bottom), courtesy youtube/RRcherrypie; 81, Bryan Toro/Shutterstock; 82-83, www.album-online.com/Newscom; 82, Ornothopter Wings. From the Codex Atlanticus, fol. 311 verso., Leonardo DaVinciArt Resource, NY; 83, Solent News/Rex USA; 84, Florian Graner/npl/Minden Pictures; 86, iStockphoto; 87, iStockphoto; 88-89, J.L. Klein & M.L. Hubert/Biosphoto; 90, The Protected Art Archive/Alamy; 91, Evgeniya Uvarova/Shutterstock; 92 (left), Eric Isselée/Shutterstock; 92 (right), bloomua/Shutterstock; 93, Premaphotos/NPL/Minden Pictures; 95 (bottom, right), Charles Brutlag/Shutterstock; 95 (bottom center, right), DenisNata/Shutterstock; 95 (top), Lisa F. Young/Shutterstock; 96 (right), Reinhard Dirscherl/SeaPics.com; 96 (top, left), Heidi & Hans-Jürgen Koch; 96 (left, center), Constantinos Petrinos/naturepl.com; 96 (bottom, left), Robert Yin/SeaPics.com; 97, NASA; 98, Odilon Dimier/Alltopress/Newscom; 100, Steshkin Yevgeniy/Shutterstock; 100-101, Doc White/SeaPics.com; 102, Iakov Kalinin/Shutterstock; 104, Aurora Creative/Getty Images; 105, Cyril Ruoso/Biosphoto; 106-107, kritskaya/Shutterstock; 108, Givaga/Shutterstock; 109, Jim Thompson/ZUMA Press/Corbis; 112 (top, front), AFP/Getty Images/Newscom; 112 (top, background), iStockphoto; 112-113 (background), iStockphoto; 112 (bottom), Piotr Naskrecki/Minden Pictures; 113 (bottom), courtesy Quick Restaurants France; 119, Franco Tempesta; 121 (left), Jonathan Bird/Getty Images; 121 (right), AP Images/Vincent Yu; 122, AP Photo/Charles Dharapak/Corbis; 124-125, courtesy Andreas Vandenberg Project, thesinkingworld.com; 127, Simon Perkin/Alamy; 128, Getty Images; 130, iStockphoto; 133, AP Photo/Geert Vanden Wijngaert; 136, AP Images/NASA; 142-143, iStockphoto; 144, iStockphoto; 145, courtesy imgur; 148, Eric Isselée/iStockphoto; 149, dien/Shutterstock; 150, Frogstar/Shutterstock; 152, Skynavin/Shutterstock; 154 (left), Eric Isselée/Shutterstock; 154 (right), Eric Isselée/Shutterstock; 155, Jay Goebel/Alamy; 156 (background), Martin Maun/Shutterstock; 156 (inset), Debra James/Shutterstock; 160-161, Alexander Demyanenko/Shutterstock; 166, Michael Sewell Visual Pursuit/Getty Images; 169, Michael Poliza/National Geographic Creative; 170, Eric Isselée/iStockphoto; 172, AFP/Getty Images/Newscom; 175, Norbert Wu/Minden Pictures; 176, Roman Samokhin/Shutterstock; 177, AP Images/Jeff Barnard; 178-179, Hiroya Minakuchi/Minden Pictures; 180, iStockphoto; 181 (left), Andrew N Dierks/iStockphoto; 181 (left, inset), iStockphoto; 181 (right), Richard Mann/Shutterstock; 183, Sarah Fields Photography/Shutterstock; 184, courtesy San Diego County Fair; 187, Tanawat Pontchour/Shutterstock; 188, Gelpi JM/Shutterstock; 188 (top), AlexRoz/Shutterstock; 189, Agustin Esmoris/Shutterstock; 190-191, Lil' Wolf/Flikr; 192, EuroPics/Newscom; 194, courtesy Car Music Project, Bill Milbrodt; 195, andersphoto/Shutterstock; 196-197, Jean-Paul Ferrero/Auscape/Minden Pictures; 198, SharkMitigation.com; 199, Shane Gross/Shutterstock

The National Geographic Society is one of the world's largest nonprofit scientific and educational organizations. Founded in 1888 to "increase and diffuse geographic knowledge," the Society works to inspire people to care about the planet. National Geographic reflects the world through its magazines, television programs, films, music and radio, books, DVDs, maps, exhibitions, live events, school publishing programs, interactive media and merchandise. *National Geographic* magazine, the Society's official journal, published in English and 32 local-language editions, is read by more than 35 million people each month. The National Geographic Channel reaches 310 million households in 34 languages in 165 countries. National Geographic Digital Media receives more than 13 million visitors a month. National Geographic has funded more than 10,000 scientific research, conservation, and exploration projects and supports an education program promoting geographic literacy.

Visit nationalgeographic.com.

For more information, please call
1-800-NGS LINE (647-5463), or
write to the following address:
National Geographic Society
1145 17th Street N.W.
Washington, D.C. 20036-4688 U.S.A.

Published by the National Geographic Society
John M. Fahey, *Chairman of the Board and Chief Executive Officer*
Declan Moore, *Executive Vice President; President, Publishing and Travel*
Melina Gerosa Bellows, *Publisher, Chief Creative Officer, Books, Kids, and Family*

Prepared by the Book Division
Hector Sierra, *Senior Vice President and General Manager*
Nancy Laties Feresten, *Senior Vice President, Kids Publishing and Media*
Jennifer Emmett, *Vice President, Editorial Director, Kids Books*
Eva Absher-Schantz, *Design Director, Kids Publishing and Media*
Jay Sumner, *Director of Photography, Kids Publishing*
R. Gary Colbert, *Production Director*
Jennifer A. Thornton, *Director of Managing Editorial*

Staff for This Book
Robin Terry, Ariane Szu-Tu, *Project Editors*
Eva Absher-Schantz, *Art Director*
Rachael Hamm Plett, Moduza Design, *Designer*
Hillary Leo, *Associate Photo Editor*
Julie Beer, Michelle Harris, *Researchers*
Callie Broaddus, *Design Production Assistant*
Margaret Leist, *Photo Assistant*
Grace Hill, *Associate Managing Editor*
Joan Gossett, *Production Editor*
Lewis R. Bassford, *Production Manager*
Susan Borke, *Legal and Business Affairs*
Paige Towler, *Editorial Intern*

Based on the "Weird But True" department in *National Geographic Kids* magazine

Production Services
Phillip L. Schlosser, *Senior Vice President*
Chris Brown, *Vice President, Book Manufacturing*
George Bounelis, *Senior Production Manager*
Nicole Elliott, *Director of Production*
Rachel Faulise, *Manager*
Robert L. Barr, *Manager*
Darrick McRae, *Imaging Technician*